Handbook of Positive

CW00504744

About the Author

Fredrike Bannink is a clinical psychologist. She has a therapy, training, coaching, and mediation practice in Amsterdam, The Netherlands. She is a trainer/supervisor with the Dutch Association for Behavioural and Cognitive Therapies (VGCt) and cofounder and Chair of the Association's Solution-Focused Cognitive Behavioural Therapy Section. She is a lecturer and supervisor at various postgraduate institutes. In addition, she provides numerous in-company training courses in solution-focused brief therapy and positive psychology at mental health care institutions; for companies, she organizes solution-focused coaching and leadership trajectories. She is also a Mental Health Trainer for Doctors Without Borders.

Fredrike Bannink is a Master of Dispute Resolution and an International Full Certified ADR Mediator. She is an international author, keynote speaker, and trainer.

Since 2005 she has been writing and presenting worldwide on the topic of bridging traditional models with positive psychology and the solution focus. Not surprisingly, her signature strength (according to the Values in Action [VIA] Survey) is *curiosity and interest in the world*.

Handbook of Positive Supervision

for Supervisors, Facilitators, and Peer Groups

Fredrike Bannink

Library of Congress Cataloging-in-Publication Data
is available via the Library of Congress Marc Database under the LC Control Number 2014952547

National Library of Canada Cataloguing in Publication Data
Bannink, Fredrike, author
    Handbook of positive supervision : for supervisors, facilitators, and
peer groups / Fredrike Bannink.

Includes bibliographical references.
Issued in print and electronic formats.
ISBN 978-0-88937-465-2 (pbk.).--ISBN 978-1-61676-465-4 (pdf).--
ISBN 978-1-61334-465-1 (html)

    1. Supervision of employees--Psychological aspects--Handbooks,
manuals, etc. 2. Positive psychology--Handbooks, manuals, etc.
I. Title. II. Title: Positive supervision.

HF5549.B25 2014   658.3'02   C2014-906831-X
                                           C2014-906832-8

The present volume is an adaptation of F. Bannink, *Positieve supervisie en intervisie* (2012,
ISBN 978-90-79729-68-5), published under licence from Hogrefe Uitgevers BV, The Netherlands.

PUBLISHING OFFICES
USA: Hogrefe Publishing Corporation, 38 Chauncy Street, Suite 1002, Boston, MA 02111
               Phone (866) 823-4726, Fax (617) 354-6875;
               E-mail customerservice@hogrefe.com
EUROPE: Hogrefe Publishing GmbH, Merkelstr. 3, 37085 Göttingen, Germany
               Phone +49 551 99950-0, Fax +49 551 99950-111; E-mail publishing@hogrefe.com

SALES & DISTRIBUTION
USA: Hogrefe Publishing, Customer Services Department,
               30 Amberwood Parkway, Ashland, OH 44805
               Phone (800) 228-3749, Fax (419) 281-6883; E-mail customerservice@hogrefe.com
UK: Hogrefe Publishing, c/o Marston Book Services Ltd., 160 Eastern Ave.,
               Milton Park, Abingdon, OX14 4SB, UK
               Phone +44 1235 465577, Fax +44 1235 465556; E-mail direct.orders@marston.co.uk
EUROPE: Hogrefe Publishing, Merkelstr. 3, 37085 Göttingen, Germany
               Phone +49 551 99950-0, Fax +49 551 99950-111; E-mail publishing@hogrefe.com

OTHER OFFICES
CANADA: Hogrefe Publishing, 660 Eglinton Ave. East, Suite 119-514, Toronto, Ontario, M4G 2K2
SWITZERLAND: Hogrefe Publishing, Länggass-Strasse 76, CH-3000 Bern 9

Hogrefe Publishing
Incorporated and registered in the Commonwealth of Massachusetts, USA, and in Göttingen, Lower Saxony,
Germany

Cover design: Daniel Kleimenhagen, Designer AGD

Printed and bound in the USA

ISBN 978-0-88937-465-2 (print) • ISBN 978-1-61676-465-4 (PDF) • ISBN 978-1-61334-465-1 (EPUB)
http://doi.org/10.1027/00465-000

Table of Contents

Preface

Suppose you are hungry and decide to go eat at a restaurant. After you have waited awhile, you are invited to take a seat. The waiter introduces himself and starts asking you questions about your hunger. How severe is your hunger; where does the appetite stem from, how long have you been hungry and have you been hungry before? What role has your hunger played in your life and your family or relationships. What disadvantages and perhaps advantages does it have for you?

After getting even hungrier the waiter wants you to fill out some questionnaires about hunger (and other issues the waiter considers important). And after all this you are served a dinner that you did not choose yourself, but rather one that the waiter claims is good for you and has helped other hungry visitors to satisfy their appetite. What do you suppose the chances are that you will leave this restaurant satisfied?

Research shows that monkeys learn more from their successes than their mistakes (Histed, Pasupathy, & Miller, 2009; Bannink, 2012c). This is due to the fact that a monkey's brain constructs new neural networks when monkeys perform tasks in which they are successful. We call this neuroplasticity. In case of failures no new networks are being built. The biologists who have studied these monkeys assume that the same mechanism applies to humans. The idea that you learn the most from your mistakes is probably out-dated.

Compare this with the preparation of food. How will you ensure that, when friends or family come over for dinner, you will come up with a meal everybody will feast upon? Are you going to use the knowledge of previous failed dishes (assuming that we have all sometimes failed in preparing a dinner)? Of course you may use your knowledge: "I put too many red peppers in that dish," or "I did not put the dish in the oven long enough." But you will most probably use your knowledge about your previous successful meals, "How did I make that gorgeous dish last time? What were the ingredients that made it so successful? You may repeat this successful recipe or build upon this success and come up with some new culinary creations.

Do you find successful or unsuccessful recipes in cookbooks or on the Internet? There are some stories about how unsuccessful dishes can be repaired, but the chance that a failed result, even after repairing it, turns into a tasty dish is rather small. The conclusion is that you probably learn more from your own and others' successes than from your own and others' failures.

In traditional supervision the focus is often on unsuccessful dishes: problems, bottlenecks, failures, stagnation, and deficits and rarely or never on successes. The problem-solving paradigm is used: what is the problem (what doesn't work), what are its causes, and how may it be repaired? In positive supervision this model is replaced by the solution-building paradigm with a focus on successful dishes: what works, how does it work, and how may you build on what works?

The role of supervisors is also different: instead of being problem-solvers or trouble-shooters who are the only experts in the room, supervisors become solutions-builders; instead of giving advice supervisors ask their supervisees questions inviting them to discover their own expertise and amplify it. From a positive psychology (PP) standpoint the question is not: "What's wrong with you?" but rather: "What's right with you?" What are your values, positive character strengths, and resources? From a solution-focused (SF) viewpoint the question is not: "What doesn't work?" but rather: "What works?" An additional benefit of this model is that supervisees may also use this paradigm in working with their own clients. Positive supervision focuses on competence: notice the parallel between finding competence and working on progress, and finding and applying successful recipes as described above.

The reason for writing this book stems from my wish to improve supervision and to make it better, more meaningful, and more enjoyable for both supervisees and their supervisors, not just in the setting of training therapists, but in many other instances as well. I think supervisees should be able to look forward to their supervision, rather than fear or endure supervision sessions, as is sometimes the case. In peer supervision colleagues should be able to enjoy their sessions and each other, rather than fear criticism or feel unsafe. At the end of each session they should leave cheerfully and with a growing sense of competence, rather than an increasing feeling of uncertainty.

The job satisfaction of both supervisors and supervisees can be increased by the positive focus described in this book. Research showing that the solution-building paradigm reduces burnout among professionals may also be relevant for supervisees and supervisors (Visser, 2012; Medina & Beijebach, 2014).

> ❝ Assuming that you are learning a profession where your passion lies, supervision is also a place to share enthusiasm for the profession. In this way supervision becomes a fun part of the training, and experiencing a shared passion creates more meaning in your work. I literally felt the urge to run to the supervision sessions to share new developments and my growth with my supervisor. After enthusiastically sharing an applied technique she once remarked: 'Who do you think was more surprised that it worked out so well, you or your client? ❞

What can you find in this book? The theoretical background and practical applications of positive supervision are outlined. There is an extensive discussion about the theory of the four pillars of positive supervision: goal formulation, finding competencies, working on progress, and reflection. The working relationship between supervisors and supervisees is also examined. Practical matters are discussed and there is a chapter containing 22 frequently asked questions and answers. In the book are also dozens of case studies, exercises, and stories. Moreover five supervisees speak out and share their experiences with positive supervision.

This book is intended for everyone who holds the role of supervisor in business or in government, for example, a senior who provides supervision to a junior colleague or trainee. This book is written for everyone in the field of psychotherapy, coaching, and conflict management who provides supervision to colleagues. It is intended for everyone who provides supervision in education or in sports, for example, a teacher who helps a student or a coach who supervises a pupil. This book is also intended for supervisees who may surprise their supervisors by giving them this book as a present, saying: "Look, there is now positive supervision!" All colleagues in peer supervision may use this book to increase their capacities and job satisfaction.

This book is intended for everyone who is dissatisfied with the current state of the art of supervision. And finally it is written for everyone who is curious enough to investigate where the concept of positive supervision may lead.

This book aims to inspire you to expand your existing proficiency and optimally deploy your creative powers to help your supervisees and colleagues to help their clients. I hope you enjoy this book and invite you to share your comments at solutions@fredrikebannink.com or through my website at www.fredrikebannink.com.

Fredrike Bannink
August 2014

Acknowledgments

An author never writes a book alone. It is always a product of many people who work together and ultimately ensure that the name of the author appears on the cover.

I thank my husband for giving me the opportunity and encouragement to write my books. I thank my many teachers and supervisors, clients, colleagues, supervisees, and students at home and abroad for all the instructive and great moments we shared and for their inspiration.

No need to say I did not invent all practical applications mentioned in this book: many of them come from my colleagues and students. Because it is impossible to thank everyone personally, I would like to thank them in this way.

I also thank my Dutch editor Erik Faas for making beautiful plans together resulting in the publication of some of my books while drinking cappuccino's, and my English editor Robert Dimbleby who didn't mind meeting me in loud bars and having dinner with me on sunny terraces. And I thank both translators Hidde Kuiper and Suzanne Aldis Routh for doing such a fine job.

Also grazie to my three Italian cats for keeping me company during many pleasant hours of thinking and writing.

Part I
Theory

Chapter 1
Supervision

Never do for learners what they can do
themselves or for themselves
Anonymous

In this chapter some definitions of traditional supervision models are described. These models are all based on the problem-solving paradigm, with the purpose of first analyzing what is wrong and then solving it (mostly about the problems supervisees have with their clients). The supervisees will usually get advice from their supervisors who position themselves as experts and teachers.

In the new vision of *positive supervision* the problem-solving paradigm is replaced by the solution-building paradigm. The supervisors usually don't give advice, but ask questions to invite their supervisees to discover and use their own expertise. This positive vision can be used both in individual and group supervision, as well as in peer supervision. Moreover, in this way supervisees may become familiar with this positive paradigm, which they may use in working with their own clients. Differences between the questions used in traditional and positive supervision are discussed, as well as a questionnaire for supervisors. Advantages and disadvantages of individual and group supervision are outlined and arguments are given to better listen to the wishes of supervisees than has hitherto been the case.

Traditional Supervision: Definition and Role of the Supervisor

Bernard and Goodyear (2009, p. 7) provide a common neutral definition of supervision. The term *neutral* means that they are not clear whether supervision is about solving problems or building solutions. Their definition reads:

Supervision is an intervention provided by a more senior member of a profession to a more junior member or members of that same profession. This relationship:

- is evaluative and hierarchical;
- extends over time;
- has the simultaneous purpose of enhancing the professional functioning of the more junior person(s), monitoring the quality of the professional services offered to the clients that she, he, or they see; and serving as a gatekeeper for those who are to enter the particular profession.

According to Bernard and Goodyear, there are major similarities between the process of psychotherapy and supervision. They state that the centrality and the role of the interpersonal relationship are similar in both processes. The outcome of psychotherapy seems to me, however, to be different from that of supervision. In psychotherapy the relationship is terminated when the clients are functioning better, while in supervision the relationship as colleagues remains.

Below I list some other definitions of supervision I found on the Internet, sometimes problem-focused, sometimes neutral. Problem-focused means that supervision is about analyzing what is wrong and then fixing those problems:

- Systematic guidance: learning from the problems the supervisee is faced with in his work (problem-focused).
- Steering, managerial superintendence (neutral).
- Reflection on (own) work experiences to achieve better functioning (neutral).

The most quoted definition of professional counseling supervision is that of Inskipp and Proctor (1995):

> A working alliance between a supervisor and a counselor in which the counselor can offer an account or recording of her work; reflect on it; receive feedback, and where appropriate, guidance. The object of this alliance is to enable the counselor to gain in ethical competence, confidence and creativity so as to give her best possible service to her clients. (p. 11)

Inskipp and Proctor (1993) suggest that supervision has three main roles; the normative, i.e., a review of supervisee practice in line with professional and ethical norms; the formative, i.e., a learning component designed to stretch the supervisee's boundaries; and the restorative, i.e., a supportive element designed to monitor and maintain supervisee self-care.

These definitions also clarify the difference between supervision and peer supervision: in supervision there is a more experienced professional who guides and supports the supervisee, creating insights; in peer supervision participants are all equals. In the above definitions supervision is a learning experience under the guidance of a supervisor (one is supposed to learn from practical problems), which methodically discusses the personal learning questions that one has with regard to his or her work. It gives insight into which situations may cause problems, what causes are involved, how to deal with the situation, and what the alternatives are. Supervisees explore and recognize patterns and search for deeper motives and beliefs that influence their actions.

According to Beunderman and Van der Maas (2011, p. 23) the supervisor is – at least in mental health care – a:

- *teacher*: teaching the profession and method to the supervisees, building on their knowledge and skills;
- *didactic person*: knowing how to transfer knowledge so that the supervisees can put it into practice;
- *expert*: having knowledge of "the state of the art" of the profession and its methods, keeps practical, scientific, and theoretical knowledge up to date, and carries out the professional standards;
- *theorist*: explaining the background of the method or the profession, has greater breadth and depth of understanding of the subject matter, and can devise links between different fields as well as between theory and practice;
- *personal coach*: discussing with the supervisees their strong points and weaknesses, personal traits and skills that have an influence on the execution of the profession, the use of the method, and the relationship with the client;
- *assessor*: assessing the performance of the supervisees with regard to the technical and methodological aspects of their field.

Watkins (1997) also indicates that the supervisor has different roles and that the success of the supervision depends primarily on the supervisor's correct estimation of when and how to apply the changing roles of mentor, teacher, and colleague.

The *problem-solving paradigm* has become popular in the medical and mechanical world and in business, government, education, psychotherapy, coaching, and (conflict) management. The focus is on what's wrong, on pathology. Diagnosis of the problem is the first step. The next step is finding the causes of the problem, using the cause-effect model (the so-called *medical model* or *mechanical model*). The problem-solving model is very straightforward: identify the cause and remove it. And indeed analyze the problem, find the cause and put it right, is a simple and attractive idiom. It makes sense and it is action-oriented. But unfortunately is it inadequate for a number of reasons:

- In a complex interactive situation we may never be able to isolate one cause;
- There is a danger in fastening on to a particular cause, because it is easy to identify, ignoring the rest of the situation;
- We may identify the cause, but cannot remove it;

- The sometimes false notion that once the cause is removed the problem will be solved and things will be back to normal, which is not usually the case.

Problem-solving certainly has a place in psychotherapy, supervision, and other areas. The main limitation, however, is that we may put much too definite a view on what we believe the solution should be before we have really done our thinking about the matter. As soon as we say "this is the problem" we have defined the sort of solution we expect.

The solution-building paradigm goes beyond reducing or repairing a problem, it is about *designing a positive outcome* that was not there before. De Bono, probably best known for his term *thinking outside the box*, states:

> With design there is a sense of purpose and a sense of fit. Problem analysis is always looking back at what is already there; design is always looking forward at what might be created. We need to design outcomes. I do not even like saying design 'solutions' because this implies that there is a problem. Even when we cannot find a cause, or, after finding it, cannot remove it, we can always attempt to design an outcome. (de Bono, 1985, p. 42)

" In problem-focused supervision I learned from the 'sharp minds' of my supervisors; in positive supervision I learned to use my own 'sharp mind.' This helps me to become more independent and more effective in creating and supporting change. "

Positive Supervision: Definition and Role of the Supervisor

In problem-focused supervision the supervisors adapt the role of *troubleshooters*, with the task as experts and teachers to give advice about the problems supervisees encounter (with their clients). Not all supervisors find this a pleasant way of supervising, especially as the responsibility is put mainly on their shoulders: after all they are the experts who have to come up with the right analyses, hypotheses, and advice.

There is a growing interest in a different view of psychotherapy and education, which is also applicable in supervision. In this view, the focus is not on what is not working and needs to be repaired, but is on what works and can be further built upon. The focus is on the strengths of supervisees instead of on their weaknesses and on their competencies instead of their deficits. The attitude of the supervisors is as follows: instead of being the only experts in the room they invite their supervisees to become coexperts and discover their own ideas and competences for optimal functioning.

In positive supervision supervisors have a stance of *not-knowing* (asking questions instead of giving advice) and *leading from one step behind*. So supervisors are in effect leading, but they stay so to speak always one step behind their supervisees. By asking questions supervisors invite their supervisees to look for their preferred future (at work) and what works to get there. Being curious about how supervisees work instead of holding a position of self-assurance, in which supervisors bring forward their own ideas, supervisors facilitate their supervisees to increase their competence. Therefore, supervisors have a more facilitating than advisory role (see Table 1). In Chapter 2 information on this new and radically different approach to health care and supervision is described in more detail.

Case 1 Well Done

A supervisor in a company explains what he is doing differently now when his employees submit an incomplete report. "I make sure to start commenting on what the employee has done well and only then I ask what further information (s)he needs to improve the report even more."

This supervisor now sends out a different message about the competencies and capabilities of his employees to make a valuable contribution to the organization than the traditional method of supervision, which focuses on mistakes or failures and how to avoid or repair them.

The following example demonstrates the philosophy and process of positive supervision. A documentary was made about how American Indians make traditional flutes from the branch of a tree. The Indian said: "The branch tells me how to cut the flute … every piece of wood has its own form, which you should respect. In each branch a flute is hidden, and it's my job to find it."

De Jong and Berg (2002, p. 268) stress that the role of supervisors is one of solutions-builders rather than problem-solvers. They base their ideas on the following set of assumptions to teach their supervisees, act as their mentor, and to feed and inspire them.

"Until proven otherwise, we assume that all supervisees:
- want to feel that their work makes *a difference* in someone's life;
- want to learn the skills needed to achieve this motivation and commitment;
- want to be accepted and valued by the organization they work in;

- want to identify with the organization's mission and objectives;
- already possess problem-solving skills to some degree; thus the task of supervision is to add solution-building skills;
- will when they feel respected and supported by the organization and their superiors, naturally deal with their clients in the same respectful manner."

Although some of the details of supervision may vary from setting to setting based on practice matters specific to those settings, the core element of any supervision is the task of the supervisors to lead their supervisees toward greater competence and enhanced skills. De Jong and Berg believe this is best accomplished through solution-building conversations that lead both supervisors and supervisees to discoveries about how they are using, and can further draw upon, their particular strengths and resources to most effectively do the work.

The most important task of supervision is to teach supervisees to listen to the clients' view of how useful the service is to them. Conversations are organized around inviting supervisees to see clients through the clients' own eyes, rather than theirs. This touches on the question whose perspective is most important in the working relationship with their clients: the perspective of the supervisees or the perspective of their clients?

In positive supervision the answer to this question is the perspective of the clients: "What would your client say her goal is?" or 'What will your clients say has been most helpful so far?" (see Chapter 6 and 8).

Analogous to this view, it is equally important for supervisors to listen to their supervisees: "What would your supervisee say her goal is?" or "What will your supervisees say has been most helpful in their supervision?"

Colleagues or institutions should not only do the assessment of supervisors, but first and foremost supervisees themselves. Supervisors and fellow reviewers should judge the performance of the supervisors more often from the perspective of their supervisees than is the case in most assessments today.

Here you find a questionnaire for assessing supervisors based on the supervisees' perspective (see Appendix 7).

1. What would your supervisees say about what you do to help them to function optimally?
2. What else would they say? And what else?
3. What difference do your supervisees say you make for them?
4. What would your supervisees say about how useful the sessions have been so far on a scale from 10–0 (10 is the most useful and 0 is the opposite)?
5. What would they say about where they are on the scale (and not lower)?
6. What would they say will be different and what would they say you will be doing differently at one or two points higher on that scale?

7. How can you get higher on the scale according to them?
8. What would they say has been most useful and helpful in your work
    with them?

Exercise 1   Positive Opening

Always start an individual or group supervision with a positive opening. Invite supervisees to briefly mention a recent (small) success or an accomplishment of which they
are proud. Another form is a short round with the question: "What are you pleased
about (at work or at home)?" This increases the chance that the rest of the session will
develop in a positive atmosphere. Don't make judgments: everything is accepted and
is given compliments by the other participants.

Sometimes the question is put forward whether positive supervision can be
integrated with problem-focused supervision. The answer depends on what
is meant by integration. The answer is negative when one tries to fit the positive vision in the problem-focused vision. The answer is positive when one
uses positive vision next to the problem-focused vision (see Chapter 10 and
Appendix 8).

Problem-Focused and Solution-Focused Questions

Grant and O'Connor (2010) did research on the differences between problem-
focused and solution-focused questions in a coaching context. Their research
shows that both types of questions are helpful in bringing the client's goal
closer, with solution-focused questions having a significantly larger effect than
problem-focused questions. Problem-focused questions reduce negative affect
and increase self-efficacy, however, they do not increase understanding of the
nature of the problem or enhance positive affect. Solution-focused questions
increase positive affect, decrease negative affect, increase self-efficacy as well
as increase participants' insight and understanding of the nature of the problem. Grant and O'Connor conclude that solution-focused questions in coaching are more effective than problem-focused questions.

During the French Revolution an attorney, a physician, and an engineer
were sentenced to death. When the day of their execution arrived, the
attorney was first onto the platform that supported the guillotine. "Blindfold or no blindfold?" asked the executioner. The attorney, not wanting

to be seen as fearful or cowardly in the face of death, held his head high and answered: "No blindfold." "Head up or head down?" continued the executioner. "Head up," said the attorney proudly. The executioner swung his ax, severing the rope that held the razor-sharp blade at the top of the scaffold. The blade dropped swiftly between the shafts and stopped just half an inch above the attorney's neck. "I am sorry' said the executioner. "I checked it just this morning. This should not have happened."

The attorney seized on the opportunity. "I think'"he addressed the executioner, "if you check The Procedural Manual For Execution By Guillotine, you will find there is a clause that states that if the guillotine malfunctions, the condemned is permitted to walk free." The executioner checked his manual, found the attorney to be correct, and set him free.

The doctor was the next to be led to the platform. "Blindfold or no blindfold?" asked the executioner. "No blindfold' said the doctor as proudly as the attorney. "Head up or head down?" asked the executioner. "Head up" said the doctor standing tall and defiant. The executioner swung his ax, cutting the rope cleanly. Once again the blade stopped just half an inch above the doctor's neck. "I can't believe this' exclaimed the executioner. "Twice in a row! I checked it out thoroughly this morning, but rules are rules and I have to abide by them. Like the attorney, your life has been spared and you may go."

The engineer was the third to mount the stand. By this time, the executioner had double-checked the guillotine and everything looked operational. "Blindfold or no blindfold?" he asked the engineer. "No blindfold"came the reply. "Head up or head down?" asked the executioner. "Head up"said the engineer. For the third time, the executioner swung back his ax to slash the rope. Just as he was about to bring the blow forward and severe the line, the engineer called out "Stop! I think I see the problem." He paid dearly for analyzing the problem.

Source: Unknown

Table 1. Differences in questions in traditional and positive supervision

Traditional supervision	Positive supervision
What went wrong?	What went right (even just a little bit)?
What is the problem?	How is this a problem (for you, for others)?
What is the cause of the problem?	Who/what can help to solve the problem?
What is wrong here (problem analysis)?	What would you like to have instead of the problem (goal analysis)?
When is the problem there and what are the consequences (functional behavior analysis of problems)?	When are/were there exceptions to the problem and what are the consequences (positive functional behavior analysis)?
What do you want to get away from?	Where do you want to go to?
Who is to blame?	Who has a solution?
What is the worst aspect of this situation?	What should be different in the future?
What is the worst that can happen?	What is the best that can happen?
Why did you do that?	How did you know you had to do that?
How did you end up in this situation?	How can you get out of this situation?
What is your explanation for your behavior?	You must have a good reason for your behavior, please tell me more?
What should you have done?	What could you do differently next time?
Can you do that more often?	How can you ensure this happens more often?
What did you try before?	What did you do before that was helpful (even just a little bit)?
Did you do something helpful?	What did you do that was helpful?
Are you committed enough?	How can you commit yourself enough?
What do you find difficult?	What do you see as a challenge?
Which obstacles do you meet?	What can you do so it may happen again?
What is stopping you?	Which (small) signals will tell you that you are on the right track?
What do you want to learn?	What do you want to become better at?
Did you ever succeed in doing better?	When did you do better?
Anything else?	What else?
Was this useful for you?	How was this useful for you?

Exercise 2 Asking Questions

Do the following exercise with another person/colleague to experience the differences between problem-focused and solution-focused questions. For 5 minutes talk to the other person about a problem, worry, or annoyance you experience. Ask the other person to respond in a problem-focused way. This involves questions such as: "How long have you experienced this?"; "How severe is it?"; "How much does it bother you?"; "What else is troubling you?"; "In what other areas of your life does this problem affect you?"; "Did you experience this before?"

Then talk to the same person for another 5 minutes about the same problem, worry, or annoyance and ask the other person to respond in a solution-focused way. This involves questions such as: "How does this present a problem for you?"; "What have you already done about it that was helpful?"; "When is the problem absent or less?"; "How do you manage that?"; "What are you doing differently then?"; "If you experienced a similar problem in the past, how did you solve it at the time?"; "What do you know about how others would address this problem?" You may also ask a question about goal formulation: "What would you like to have accomplished by the end of this (brief) conversation so that you would be able to say that it has been of use to you and that it was meaningful?"

With the other person note the differences between the two conversations. You may sense a lighter tone and be in a more optimistic mood when you talk about the more positive experiences, whereas a certain heaviness often accompanies problem-focused conversations. It is also possible that you have already solved your problem or that you know what to do in order to reach your goal.

Then reverse roles: now you listen while the other person talks about a problem, worry, or annoyance. For the first 5 minutes, respond in a problem-focused way, and then for the next 5 minutes in a solution-focused way. With the other person, note the differences again.

" I am pleased that positive supervision complimented my heavy problem-oriented approach. The result is that I now have a multi-colored palette of approaches available to me. And if nowadays I want to unravel problems again, I focus much more on analyzing situations where the problem doesn't exist. I noticed that this is a pleasant way of working for my clients. I do hope that other supervisees will experience the same as I did through this book. "

Individual Supervision and Group Supervision

Supervision can take place both individually and in groups. Both types have advantages and disadvantages. Advantages of individual supervision are the exclusive attention for supervisees. Individual supervision is often experienced as safer and more confidential than group supervision. Disadvantages include that dependence can develop towards the supervisor or that more transference and countertransference may happen (see Chapter 8).

According to Proctor and Inskipp (2001) in group supervision four types can be distinguished, often depending on the level of competence of the supervisees:

- Authoritative supervision – the supervisor, treating the group members as a more or less participative audience, supervises each member one-to-one;
- Participative supervision – the supervisor negotiates with members to help them become skilled and active participants in the work of supervision – hence supervision *with* a group;
- Cooperative supervision – set up in such a way that the supervisor is the facilitator and wicket-keeper for the group members sharing fully in each other's supervision;
- Peer group supervision – members share the full responsibility of supervisor for each other and negotiate how leadership will be shared.

Benefits of group supervision are that it is usually cheaper than individual supervision and supervisees share information and may learn from each other. Disadvantages include that working in a group can be experienced as unsafe or there might be less attention when it is another supervisee's turn or when another supervisee demands a lot of attention.

Supervisees' Wishes

I believe that perhaps the most important task in supervision is to ensure that the dignity of the supervisees and their clients is maintained. Positive supervision is consistent with the wishes of supervisees. Worthen and McNeill (1996) argue that little attention is paid to the needs and wishes of supervisees. Also Beunderman and Van der Maas (2011) indicate that the question is whether the expectations of the supervisors in the supervision process always match with the wishes and needs of the supervisees. This may be due to a disagreement about what constitutes good supervision. What supervisors regard as positive in the development of the supervisees can be perceived as negative by the supervisees, or vice versa. It appears that supervisors are not so much concerned with the ambition of their future colleagues to succeed, but mainly focus on the fears and insecurities of their supervisees such as shame and uncertainty about their approach (Van der Linden, 1993). This may lead to dissatisfaction, anxiety, or conflicts (see Chapters 9 and 11).

Thomas (1996) describes research done by Heath and Tharp (1991) in which they examined the supervision process in an attempt to build understanding of therapists' needs, desires, and requirements. The six themes that developed from this research seem particularly relevant to the discussion of supervision models that utilize positive approaches. This is what supervisees want to tell their supervisors:

1. We want relationships based on mutual respect;
2. You don't have to be a guru;
3. Supervise us or evaluate us; not both;
4. Assume that we're competent. We're hard enough on ourselves already;
5. Tell us what we're doing right. Affirm us. Empower us;
6. Listen to us. Make supervision a human experience.

Exercise 3   Success, Talent, Ambition

As a way of introduction, invite group members to talk in pairs for 3 minutes each about their successes, talents, and ambitions. Then invite each group member to give a short (1 minute each) introduction of their partner to the rest of the group making use of the successes, talents, and ambitions they just shared. In this way this exercise is also useful to train their listening skills.

Definitions of Peer Supervision

Most definitions of peer supervision found on the Internet are problem-focused:

- A meeting at work on the basis of the exchange of experience and knowledge, where problems and issues are addressed.
- An organized discussion between people working in or training in the same field of work. Conversations are about activities and their related problems. The aim is enhancing the expertise of those involved and the quality of work.
- A form of enhancement of expertise in which people appeal to their colleagues to think about personal and job-related issues and problems. Within a peer group there should be no hierarchy.
- Discussing problems at work in a group of equals.

Neutral definitions of peer supervision I found in the dictionary are:
- Consultation between colleagues who do not work in the same job or office.
- Peer consultation groups provide a forum for practitioners to meet informally with peers and colleagues to discuss clinical and practice issues in a supportive and confidential setting.
- Arrangements in which peers work together for mutual benefit are referred to as peer supervision or peer consultation. Peer consultation may be the more appropriate term to describe a process in which critical and supportive feedback is emphasized while evaluation is deemphasized. Consultation, in contrast to supervision, is characterized by the counselor's right to accept or reject the suggestions [of others]. Yet, the terms peer supervision and peer consultation both can be used to describe similar nonhierarchical relationships in which participants have neither the power nor the purpose to evaluate one another's performance.

As a *definition of positive peer supervision* I suggest: building solutions among peers for greater personal and methodical competence, with support and encouragement to and from each other in discussing and implementing these skills.

Peer-guided peer supervision means that a group of peers is finally able to function independently. Until then, there is guidance from a supervisor or a more experienced colleague.

Exercise 4   A Happy Life

Take 5 minutes every evening, or whenever you feel like it, to reflect on how you have been working today to build happiness for yourself and those around you. Ask yourself these three questions for a happy life. Of course these questions can also be used in your work as a supervisor and for supervisees.
- What did I do today that I feel good about?
- What has someone else done that I am happy with? Did I react in such a way that this person may do something like that again?
- What else do I see, hear, feel, smell, or taste that I am grateful for?

In my country, The Netherlands, to date the forms to be filled in to become a supervisor of the Dutch Association of Behavioural and Cognitive Therapies are problem-focused, as is the case in many other organizations. They are based on problems formulated by the clients, not by the supervisees; they are centered about giving advice and interpretations, with a focus on problems, negative emotions, weaknesses, and deficits. In Appendix 8 I propose to modify this form, which also clarifies how the problem-focused vision may well be complemented with the positive vision as described in this book. I assume the demands for training courses in other countries may also be changed, where the focus is still predominantly on problems.

Summary

- Definitions of traditional supervision focus on solving problems (mostly problems supervisees have with their clients). The role of the supervisors consists of analyzing problems and giving advice to their supervisees.
- There is a new vision in (mental) health care and other fields, using positive (peer) supervision, where the problem-solving paradigm is replaced by the solution-building paradigm. The role of the supervisors is to ask questions to invite supervisees to discover and use their expertise to perform optimally.
- (Research about) the differences between problem-focused and solution-focused questions are discussed.
- A questionnaire for supervisors (and fellow evaluators) is presented and takes the perspective of supervisees as the main starting point.
- Advantages and disadvantages of individual and group supervision are discussed.
- Supervisors should listen more to the wishes of their supervisees; they know how supervisors should behave.
- In definitions of supervision the problem-solving model is still predominant. Using positive supervision one builds on what works rather than fix what does not work.

Chapter 2
Positive Supervision

Water the flowers, not the weeds.
Fletcher Peacock

The basis for positive supervision is formed by two recent trends in psychotherapy, which share a positive focus: *positive psychology* (PP) and *solution-focused brief therapy* (SFBT). The history and principles of both will be briefly outlined.

Research in PP shows that positive emotions provide creativity, flexibility, and empathy, which are important in supervision. SFBT focuses on the desired outcome in the future instead of on the undesirable situation in the past or present. Goal formulation, a focus on what works, and signs of (further) progress are at the basis of SFBT. I developed four basic solution-focused questions, which are recognizable throughout the chapters in this book by the four pillars of positive supervision. These pillars are: goal formulation, finding competencies, working on progress, and reflection. This format differs from traditional models, in which sequential phases of supervision or phases in the development of supervisees determine the way supervision is done. This chapter concludes with a brief comparison between PP and SFBT.

Principles of Positive Supervision

In Chapter 1 a *definition of positive supervision* is presented: the guiding of supervisees to greater competence and the increase of their competencies by building solutions.

You might be wondering whether *negative* supervision exists. My answer to that question is negative. I think there is no negative supervision because all forms of supervision – including traditional problem-focused supervision – aim at helping colleagues to achieve desired changes in their lives and work. Therefore I prefer to speak of *traditional supervision* when I refer to problem-focused supervision where one focuses on repairing what is wrong instead of building on what is right.

The good news is that positive supervision does not have to be built from scratch. In some cases there is already a (unfortunately often brief) focus on what works. According to Beunderman and Van der Maas (2011, p. 59) the supervisor gives positive feedback *when needed* (italics FB). One important difference with positive supervision is that positive feedback is not just given when needed, but that this form of *positive reinforcement (operant conditioning)* is given as much and often as possible (see this Chapter and Chapter 4). The aforementioned authors discuss with the supervisees their strengths and weaknesses (p. 23). They do not clarify how those strengths are used in supervision in order to contribute to (further) progress. I will describe this in more detail in Chapter 4, discussing finding competencies and the concept of *competence transference*: how supervisees' strengths may be used to overcome problems or to function optimally.

Positive supervision is not about problem analysis, but about *goal analysis*: "What do you want to have achieved at the end of the supervision?" or "How will you know that this supervision (session) has been useful?" or "'What are your best hopes?,'" followed by "What difference will that make?"

The important question "What else?" invites supervisees to think about what else contributes to hope, difference, what works, and next steps, not only from their own perspective, but also from the perspective of others, such as their clients, colleagues, and family members. This open question suggests *that* there is more. A closed question ("Anything else?") will easily produce a negative answer because it does not invite supervisees to look any further.

Case 2 Hope and Differences

On the first question: "What are your best hopes for this supervision?" the supervisee replies that she hopes to be able to apply psychotherapy in a flexible manner, she hopes to maintain her perspective when therapy develops differently than expected, and she hopes to be able to stand firm, especially in the case of conflicts with clients or her team. She also hopes to improve in doing diagnostics, to motivate her clients more effectively to change, and to know how to make her herself no longer needed by her clients.

The supervisor then asks the second question about *positive differences*, in which also other perspectives are used: "What difference will it make *for you* if your best hopes are met at the end of the supervision?" She replies that as a result her job satisfaction will be high and she will take pride in her job. Moreover she will feel competent in her work. The difference *for her clients* will be that their emancipation will be activated, their satisfaction with the therapeutic relationship will be increased, they suffer less and feel more competent, allowing them to need less intensive treatment.

The difference *for her colleagues* will be that they will feel inspired by this way of working and thus their job satisfaction will be higher, that they can make a bigger difference for their clients, and that the team will work effectively, resulting in more appreciation from clients, colleagues, and managers.

Case 3 **Reflecting on Strengths**

At the start of a group supervision with two supervisees the supervisor asks what they both like in their work and what they are good at. Supervisee A mentions that she is good at siding with her clients instead of opposing them, she acts swiftly when needed, she is empathetic and makes an effort to help others. Supervisee B mentions that she is a good listener, is creative in searching for solutions with her clients, and shows patience and tenacity.

The supervisor then invites both supervisees to reflect on the strengths of each other; after all they work together and know each other. As strengths of A Supervisee B cites that she is firm, empathetic, and easily builds an alliance with clients and colleagues. Supervisee A describes as strengths of B that she is a quiet person, a good listener, and that she shows patience and integrity. What's nice about this question is that colleagues often will come up with other things than expected. It may come as a surprise to hear what strengths the other sees in them.

Of course positive supervision is not *problem-phobic*. Problematic issues (supervisees' own problems or problems with their clients) may be put forward. The supervisors (and colleagues in peer supervision) listen respectfully and acknowledge the fact that this problem causes them to suffer ("I understand this must be difficult for you. How do you cope?"). As soon as possible, however, the supervisors ask what the supervisees want to have instead of the problem. The supervisors do not ask for details of the problem (of the supervisees or their clients).

Often supervisees think that it is necessary to tell in detail what is wrong with their clients and that the supervisors will provide suggestions or advice about the diagnosis and/or approach, as is common in traditional problem-focused supervision. Sometimes supervisees have to get used to the idea that they are invited to talk about their own ideas about what works. Supervisors should not think too quickly that supervisees have no clue or do not possess the necessary competences!

In positive supervision the supervisors don't need to know much about the story of the clients. The main focus is not on the clients of the supervisees, but on finding competencies, skills, creative ideas, and strengths of the supervisees themselves, and to support supervisees as much as possible to use these abilities, qualities, ideas, and strengths in working with their clients. This vision can also to be found in the models for reflection described in Chapter 6. For example: without the supervisees first explaining a stagnating case the supervisors ask what the supervisees will have done differently when at the end of the next session with the client the supervisees rates the alliance a point higher than the last session on a scale of 10–0, with 10 meaning that the alliance is great and the client is making progress and 0 means the opposite.

"Water the flowers, not the weeds," as indicated at the start of this chapter, clearly shows the use of operant conditioning: positive supervision gives as

much *positive reinforcement* (giving attention) as possible to whatever works and as much *negative punishment* (withholding attention) as possible to everything that doesn't work. In other words, positive supervision gives positive reinforcement of *solution-talk* instead of *problem-talk*. This is different from the problem-focused model, which mainly uses respondent conditioning principles (Bannink, 2012b). One might say that in positive supervision the supervisors play the role of *cheerleaders* (de Shazer, 1988).

The supervisors don't give advice or suggestions, or only when invited to do so. Earlier we saw that the attitude of the professional is one of *not knowing* (asking questions to invite supervisees to discover and use their own expertise rather than giving them suggestions or advice) and *leading from one step behind*. If the supervisors are invited to, they may offer suggestions or advice, but only after the supervisees are first invited as coexperts to come up with their own ideas and expertise.

Finally, no assumptions or interpretations are given. De Shazer, cofounder of SFBT, states: "If you find a hypothesis coming up, take two aspirins, go to bed, and hope that tomorrow it's over." That's because hypotheses often narrow the field of vision.

This example from my work as a trainer for the Mental Health Team of Doctors without Borders clarifies the stance of "leading from one step behind" In a training course in the northern part of Sri Lanka at one point the participants wanted to discuss psychosis. After my question what their definition of psychosis is, I invited them to share what they do with these patients. "We beat them and lock them up," is their answer. At that point I could have given the advice to stop doing that, but I asked instead – after my initial shock – in what percentage of cases this strategy worked, knowing they must have a good reason for doing so and that their solutions would at least sometimes work, because this is what they have been doing for ages. And of course from their perspective they have a good reason: they think evil spirits, which they have to beat out of them, possess these people. Around 50% of the cases, is the answer. "What else is working?" is my next question. They tell me that they get lots of different medications, which work in around 30%. Again I asked, "What else?" Only after being invited to share how we in the Western world treat people with psychosis, I gave them this information. Because this their invitation and after the participants had the opportunity to share their stories about what works, they are interested in finding out my story, probably more so than when I would have given them advice from the start without their invitation. In that case I would have shown less respect for their way of thinking and doing.

Four Pillars of Positive Supervision

The four pillars of positive supervision are:
    Pillar 1: Goal formulation (Chapter 3)
    Pillar 2: Finding competencies (Chapter 4).
    Pillar 3: Working on (further) progress (Chapter 5).
    Pillar 4: Reflection (Chapter 6).

Each chapter describes a number of practical applications associated with each pillar. This designation doesn't imply, however, that these pillars can only be used in this order. Sometimes it may be necessary to return to goal formulation ("What was it again that you want to have achieved at the end of the supervision?") and finding competence is an ongoing process when working on further progress ("How were you able to do that?"). In addition, reflection is so important that this should be addressed at the end of each supervision session. Figure 1 illustrates the positive supervision process. The process can be run through the total supervision process and/or through every session.

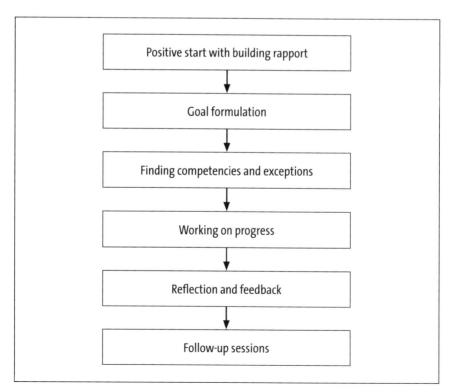

Figure 1. The positive supervision process.

- If there is progress: do more of what works/stop when the goal is reached;
- If there is no progress: stop and do something different: return to building rapport and/or goal formulation and start the process again/stop/refer (see Appendix 7).

The positive supervision process is carried out for the entire supervision and/or for each supervision session individually.

> 66 If I compare this approach of supervision with the more traditional problem-focused supervision for me the difference lies mainly in two points: the motivational effect the focus on positive cognitions and behavior has and the confidence in my own power to devise appropriate solutions. Changing the focus from an analysis of problem behavior to an analysis of positive and successful behavior and cognitions reinforces my positive emotions. It strengthens my hope of a positive outcome and my confidence that this is feasible using small steps forward. 99

Exercise 5   Helping Questions

Consider a typical problematic situation. Write down the typical questions you ask yourself or others about it. Examine these questions closely. Does asking them help you feel better or worse? Does asking them help move you forward to where you want to be or merely give you an explanation for why you are stuck or can't change? If your questions are not helping you, find some more helpful questions.

Case 4   Obligation to Make an Effort

A coaching supervisee worries whether she is doing the right things and wonders if she could have done any better. In a previous supervision the main focus had been on what she should have done differently, how clients might have become more motivated, and which of her weaknesses were involved when this didn't happen.

It is quite normal that supervisees feel hugely responsible for the results of their work and this may create a heavy burden. They are frequently so eager to see their clients change that often they start pushing and pulling their clients to ensure that something does change, usually to no effect. The results are negative emotions stemming from irritation, discouragement, or uncertainty (see Chapter 8).

I normalize her feeling responsible and explain to her that it doesn't surprise me that she experiences this as a heavy burden, especially given her experiences with her previous supervisor. I also tell her that, although she has an *obligation to make an effort*, she doesn't have the *obligation to reach a result*. She should do her best to invite her clients to change their behavior and to motivate them, but whether they actually decide to take action is up to the clients themselves. It is not unusual that supervisees forget that most clients are responsible for their own lives and their decisions. The supervisee says she feels very relieved by this explanation.

Solution-Talk

The problem-focused model uses a different language from the positive or solution-focused model. Often someone gets stuck by thinking and talking about a situation in a problem-focused way, paying much attention to the (causes in the) unwanted past. If people use a language, which demoralizes them, then hope and the chances that they may find a solution for that problem will grow smaller.

Language, however, can also promote change in how people perceive their problems. *Solution-talk*, with a focus on goals and solutions, automatically ensures choices and change. How can you use solutions-talk in supervision instead of problem-talk? Here are a few tips to use solutions-talk or invite your supervisees to do the same:

- Use the past tense when talking about problems. Say, for example: "Until now I felt insecure," instead of, "I feel insecure" or, "I will feel insecure for the rest of my life." In this way the present and the future remain open for solutions and possibilities. Use the future tense to talk about what you want instead of the problem: "How will your life look when you are feeling (more) secure?;"
- Talk about what you do want instead of what you don't want;
- Talk about the presence of something instead of the absence of it. So talk about what you can do instead of what you can't do;
- Avoid using words like "always," "never," "everybody," and "nobody." By using these words the chances of enhancing hope and creative thinking diminish. Instead of saying: "We never get along well together," say: "Most of the time we don't get along well together," leaving openings for finding exceptions;
- Do not talk about yourself or someone else as *being* the problem. Do not label people in a negative way and equate the person with his or her (psychiatric) diagnosis. Instead of saying: "He is a procrastinator" or "She is depressed," say: "He has a tendency to procrastinate" or "She is suffering from depressive episodes," leaving openings for looking at strengths and resources;

- Use language, which generates positive expectations. For example, say: "Until now I haven't found a great job" instead of "I will never get a great job." Also use *when* instead of *if*: "When I have solved this problem I will feel happier" instead of: "If I have solved this problem I will feel happier." Only in the case of *relapse prevention if* is used instead of *when*: "If there would be a relapse, what is important then to keep remembering?"

Exercise 6   Percentage Solutions-Talk

The difference between traditional and positive supervision can easily be measured by the percentage of time spent in discussing strengths, resources, successes, and what works. Is it 10%? Is it 20%? Is it 50% or perhaps 0%? Suppose you were the supervisee, how would you like this percentage to be? Would you like to be invited to talk about your strengths, resources, and successes? You probably would. So raise the percentage of time you normally spend by 10% (if you use 10%, make it 20%) and notice what difference this makes for your supervisees and for yourself!

Exercise 7   Problem or Opportunity

Sit comfortably, close your eyes or ask your supervisees to do this exercise, and repeat the following sentence ten times: "I have a big problem!" Observe closely what you are experiencing physically and emotionally. Notice the effect that this sentence has on your body and on your emotions.
Stretch a little, get up and do the exercise again. Set yourself comfortably again, close your eyes, and repeat the following sentence ten times: "I have a great opportunity!" Once again, observe the effects that this sentence has on your physical and emotional state.

Here is a variant of "Water the flowers, not the weeds," showing the importance of positive reinforcement. A Native American elder once described his own inner struggle. "Inside of me there are two dogs. One of the dogs is mean and evil, the other dog is good. The mean dog fights the good dog all the time." When his grandson asked him which dog wins, he reflected for a moment and replied: "The dog I feed most."

Positive Psychology

So far little attention has been paid to strengths and resources in psychology and psychotherapy. This may well reflect the spirit of the age in which most disciplines such as psychology and psychiatry have focused on problems, complaints, symptoms, and deficits and how to reduce them. As an example the international literature in psychology (Psychological Abstracts) between 1970–2000 has about 54,000 articles on depression, 41,000 on anxiety, and only about 400 articles on joy (Myers, 2000). In all, there were 21 articles on negative emotions for every article on positive emotions.

Since PP was introduced in the late 1990s, psychotherapists focus increasingly not only on complaints, but also on strengths. No longer is only reducing symptoms the central focus, but now developing strengths is also. This refers to positive, functional, and health-promoting factors. Instead of concentrating on what is wrong and needs mending (see Chapter 1) the focus shifts to what is right and what factors promote the capacity of our clients. The popularity of this approach has now been scientifically supported; there is a great amount of research on many constructs of PP (as an *umbrella term*) and its *family members* such as hope, optimism, positive emotions, contentment, self-efficacy, flow, and gratitude, not only in psychotherapy, but also, for example, in general medicine (Hershberger, 2005; Bannink, 2009a, 2012a).

Seligman (2002), one of the founders of PP, became well known for his research in the 1970s on learned helplessness (the belief people have that they cannot solve their own problems). Later on he shifted his research to *learned optimism*. In his last book he presents his *well-being theory*. 'If we want to flourish and if we want to have well-being, we must indeed minimize our misery; but in addition, we must have positive emotion, meaning, accomplishment, and positive relationships. The skills and exercises that build these are entirely different from the skills that minimize our suffering' (Seligman, 2011, p 53). This theory consists of five elements, of which the first three elements were already present in his former *happiness theory*:

1. Positive emotions (the pleasant life);
2. Engagement (the engaged life);
3. Meaning (the meaningful life);
4. Positive relations;
5. Accomplishment (the pursue of success, accomplishment, winning, achievement, and mastery for its own sake).

The goal of positive psychology is to increase flourishing by increasing positive emotion (P), engagement (E), positive relationships (R), meaning (M), and accomplishment (A). A handy mnemonic is PERMA.

Positive Emotions

The same positive focus, used in positive psychotherapy, can be used in supervision. The effect of positive emotions was demonstrated by Fredrickson (2009), a researcher in the field of PP. In her *broaden and build theory of positive emotions* she states that positive emotions such as joy, pride, contentment, gratitude, hope, optimism, and love generate more creativity, flexibility, and empathy (positive emotions *broaden* the thinking) and *build* relationships, resilience, and health. They also work as an antidote for negative emotions. Isen and Reeve (2005) also demonstrate that positive emotions increase *intrinsic motivation*. Therefore, it is the task of supervisors to generate as many positive emotions as possible by asking supervisees about their desired future, competences, successes, etc. in order to enhance their creativity, flexibility, and empathy.

> Scientists examined the ways physicians make medical diagnoses by having them think aloud while they solved the case of a patient with liver disease. Astonishingly, this research team found that when they gave physicians a small gift – simply a bag of candy – those physicians were better at integrating case information and less likely to become fixated on their initial ideas, coming to premature closure in their diagnosis
>
> Source: Isen, Rosenzweig, and Young (1991)

It is important that supervisors have the capacity to be empathetic. It ensures the willingness to help others. By helping someone you put the positivity outside yourself, so to speak, and into the relationship with that other person. Just like negativity, positivity is *contagious*, because people often subconsciously imitate each other. In this case, there is a chain reaction of positivity, with people experiencing more connectedness and more compassion for each other (Isen, Daubman, & Nowicki, 1987; Gilbert, 2010). If we feel good, the willingness to help others increases. Sometimes we lose this ability: for example, in the case of *burnout*, empathy is no longer present and we cannot identify with the stories that our clients (or supervisees) tell us anymore.

Research shows that positive emotions enhance openness, flexibility, and better social relationships (Webster Nelson, 2009). Students in the USA read a story about someone from a different culture who was in trouble. When the students were in a neutral or negative mood, they sympathized less with that person and showed no empathy. Students in a positive mood (mostly by receiving a little present or some sweets) did sympathize and showed empathy for the person in trouble.

Exercise 8   Altruism Wins

Performing *acts of kindness* produces the single most reliable momentary increase in well-being of any PP exercises tested. Research shows that this will result in an increase in well-being, especially if people perform the five acts of kindness all in one day (Lyubomirsky, 2008).

Invite supervisees (and yourself) to set themselves the goal of performing five new acts of kindness in a single day (they should not do them every day, since this may become boring and less effective) over six weeks. Ask them to aim for actions that really make a difference and come at some cost to them, such as donating blood, helping a neighbor with their yard work, or figuring out a better way that their ailing father might manage his chronic pain. Ask them to make a point to carry them all out on a single day. At the end of the day invite them to notice the good feelings that come with increasing their kindness. For lasting impact, ask them to make their kindness day a recurring ritual and be creative each week. Ask them to find new ways to make a positive difference in the lives of others and try it for a few months to observe the change it makes.

It is nice to share positive events with others and this has some other advantages, as can been seen below.

Research by Gable, Reis, Impett, and Asher (2004) on capitalization, telling others about positive events in one's life, shows that this generates additional affect, over and above positive affect associated with the event itself. There are several possible mechanisms for such an effect. First, sharing a positive event with others requires retelling the event, which creates an opportunity for reliving and reexperiencing the event. Furthermore, the communicative act may involve rehearsal and elaboration, both of which seem likely to prolong and enhance the experience by increasing its salience and accessibility in memory. In this way, capitalization builds personal and social resources.

Positivity Ratio

In physics there is a tipping point at the moment water turns to ice or vice versa. There is also a *positivity ratio,* which is the tipping point between abnormal or normal functioning and functioning very well, also called *flourishing.* Research shows that to counterbalance one negative emotion more positive emotions are necessary in order to perform well. This ratio consists of three positive emotions to one negative one (3:1), preferably even higher. If someone is doing badly (e.g., someone feels depressed) then the ratio is often even lower than 1:1. Most people have a positivity ratio of about 2:1, which means that most moments are positive, but that's not enough to really flourish.

Fredrickson researched the positivity ratio together with Losada, who developed a mathematical model about her broaden and build theory. For many years Losada researched well-performing teams. According to his mathematical research the magic positivity ratio is 2,9013:1, rounded to 3:1 (Fredrickson & Losoda, 2005). Recently there has been criticism on their model, arguing that it is based on poorly reported experiments and elementary errors in the use of differential equations. Fredrickson responded to the critique by agreeing that Losada's mathematical model is questionable and doesn't show that there are precise values of the ratio, but the evidence for the benefits of a high positivity ratio is still solid. Gottman (1994) researches partner relationships. He makes a distinction between relationships that flourish (*flourishing marriages*) and relationships that do not do well or where partners divorce. He states that to every negative or disapproving remark or signal there should be five positive remarks or signals made as counterbalance to enable a relationship to flourish. In relationships where partners divorced this ratio often dropped below 1:1, with more negative than positive emotions. Of seven hundred newlywed couples he could predict with 94% accuracy whether they would still be together ten years later by scoring a film of 15 minutes of positive and negative interactions by these couples. There is also research into the differences between *flourishing* or well-functioning teams and teams who do less well (Losada & Heaphy, 2004). In flourishing teams there is a positivity ratio of 5:1 or even 6:1 (see Table 2).

Table 2. Positivity ratio

	Positive emotions	Negative emotions
Normal individual functioning	2	1
Individual flourishing	3	1
Flourishing relationships	5	1
Flourishing teams	5–6	1

The good news is that everyone can increase their positivity ratio and may have more control over it than they might think. This applies for individual functioning, as well as in relationships with others, like a partner, children, colleagues, clients, and supervisees. But one has to put in an ongoing effort to get higher than 2:1, is doesn't come easily!

I suppose the same positivity ratio of 5:1 applies for supervision, meaning that negative emotions between supervisors and supervisees or between peers in supervision are acceptable. Sometimes supervisors may criticize the behavior of their supervisees. In turn, supervisees may indicate that their supervisors are doing things they don't like. Of course the way in which criticism is presented makes a lot of difference; criticism presented in terms of errors or mistakes may create a defensive attitude.

> **"**The previous supervisor looked at the errors and mistakes I made and at capacities, which I didn't have (yet). When my imperfections were highlighted, I always had the urge to start defending myself. This, however, was like fighting a losing battle: a mistake was a mistake and 'I should have known better. Every time I noticed that I cringed and I started even to feel anxious about the supervision sessions. Despite the fact that my clients appreciated my treatments, I grew more and more uncertain. The last months of my internship I went to my work and supervision with abdominal pain.**"**

Positive reinforcement, as a form of operant conditioning, is one of the most important tools that supervisors have at their disposal in working with supervisees. It has a positive effect on everybody irrespective of status, position, or nature of problem. Positive reinforcement helps in solving problems and it also helps in increasing the possibility that someone will feel better and maintain agreeable relationships. Material reinforcement can be used as positive reinforcement such as sweets, or an outing. Social reinforcement such as a smile, eye contact, company, compliments, or a pat on the shoulder also work. This social reinforcement is particularly effective but unfortunately underutilized in individual and peer supervision. In all kinds of social situations the golden rule applies: 5:1 is the most effective, in other words five compliments, affirmations, etc. against one disapproval, criticism, or negative remark (Flora, 2000).

There is a difference between positive reinforcement and a positive approach. One does not reinforce the person, only the behavior of that person. A positive approach to the person is also very useful and produces favorable effects, for instance on the well-being of this person. Reinforcement of behavior must closely follow that behavior if it is to be at all effective and what for one person is seen as reinforcement is not so for another. This reinforcement is not expensive, is inexhaustible, and it works, so long as there is enough variation.

Earlier we saw that in order *to flourish* a positivity ratio is required of at least 3:1. Although the positivity ratio and the above rule of thumb are not exactly the same, they will undoubtedly contribute to each other. As someone receives more positive reinforcement, the chance *to flourish* increases. However, there is a ceiling of the positivity ratio, in the U.S.A this is 11:1. If the ratio is higher, then someone gets too positive and becomes irritating and implausible. In European countries this ratio will probably be lower (see Chapter 11).

Solution-Focused Brief Therapy

Solution-Focused Brief Therapy (SFBT) was developed during the 1980s by de Shazer, Berg, and colleagues at the Brief Family Therapy Center in Milwaukee, USA. They expanded upon the findings of Watzlawick, Weakland, and Fish (1974), who found that the attempted solution would sometimes perpetuate the problem and that an understanding of the origins of the problem was not always necessary. Some propositions of de Shazer (1985) are:

- The development of a solution is not necessarily related to the problem. An analysis of the problem itself is not useful in finding solutions, whereas an analysis of exceptions to the problem is (What did you do to solve the problem that was helpful?);
- The clients are the experts. They are the ones who determine the goal and the road to achieving this. Your destination is not determined by the starting point;
- If it is not broken, do not fix it. Leave alone what is positive in the perception of the clients;
- Focus on what can be changed: focus on solutions and possibilities instead of problems and impossibilities;
- Quick changes or solution of the problem is possible and often a small change is sufficient;
- If something works (better), do more of it. Even though it may be something completely different from what was expected;
- If something does not work, do something else. More of the same leads nowhere.

A Japanese coastal village was once threatened by a tidal wave, but the wave was sighted in advance, far out on the horizon, by a lone farmer in the rice fields on the hillside above the village. There was no use in shouting and there was no time to go home to warn his people. At once he set fire to the field and the villagers who came swarming up to save their crops were saved from flood.

Psychiatrist Erickson (Rossi, 1980) also contributed to the development of SFBT. He gave students the task of reading the last page of a book and speculating about what had preceded it. SFBT similarly departs from the goal of the clients and links their preferred future to the present situation. Erickson emphasized the competence of the clients and argued that the point was not to adapt the treatment to a diagnostic classification, but to find out what possibilities for taking a (different) course of action client themselves reveal. Erickson also used the hypnotic technique of *pseudo orientation in time*. During hypnosis, he had his clients imagine running into him in 6 months and telling him that their problem had been solved and how they had achieved that. He ended the hypnosis by offering a few suggestions for the client to forget what had happened during the hypnosis. And even though they did not always apply the same solutions that they had put forward under hypnosis, it turned out that many of them reported doing better 6 months later.

Further information about (research on) SFBT can be found in Bannink (2007a, b, 2008a, 2010b, 2013) and Franklin, Trepper, Gingerich, and McCollum (2012).

> " Turning limitations into possibilities, thinking in challenges instead of problems, focusing on solutions instead of stagnation .... isn't it a bit forced? Isn't this way of looking at things just for some trippy types, not for more sober people like me? These are just a few of the prejudices I had to overcome. "

Four Basic Solution-Focused Questions

SFBT evolved from practice, whereas PP evolved from scientific studies. The staff at the Brief Family Therapy Center discovered that three specific types of therapist behavior made clients four times as likely to talk about solutions, change, and resources:

1. Asking eliciting questions: "What would you like to have instead of the problem?" or "When is the problem less or absent?"
2. Asking questions about details: "How exactly did you do that? What exactly did you do differently?"
3. Giving verbal rewards by paying compliments and asking competence questions: "How did you manage that? How did you come up with that great idea?"

Goal-formulation, positive reinforcement of what (already/still) works, and focusing on signs of (further) progress are the common thread in solution-focused interviewing. For this, I developed four basic solution-focused questions, which can be identified in the chapters in the four pillars of positive supervision (Bannink, 2009a). Questions 1 and 2 deal with goal formulation;

question 3 involves finding competence and what works; question 4 is about working on (further) progress. The four basic solution-focused questions are:
1. What are your best hopes? What else?
2. What difference will that make? What else?
3. What works? What else?
4. What will be next signs of progress? or What will be your next step? What else?

Since the 1990s, there is an interest in *solution-focused supervision*. Rudes, Shilts, and Berg (1997, p.213) argue that the same principles apply as in SFBT. Rather than focus on teaching or instructive dialog, it makes sense to focus on learning through interaction, in which the trainees become involved and curious about their own thinking about the therapy process. Such supervision is informed by the trainees' experiences and expectations rather than by an all-knowing supervisor-as-expert who attempts to rectify faulty thinking or provide a corrective experience more in line with the expert supervisor's understanding of what will help. Instead, the goal is simply to talk with trainees who are grappling with their understanding of the client system or the model being applied and to create a context in which possibilities exist to cocreate novel alternatives and new solutions. According to Rudes et al. (1997) there are some points of importance in supervision:
1. The role of the supervisor is to facilitate the supervisory conversation of the participants in an attempt to understand each supervisee's concerns and to develop a dialog that is respectful of all the participants in that context;
2. Supervisors should use curiosity as an antidote to certainty whereby they show not only interest in the perspectives of their supervisees, but also tentativeness in presenting their own views. Posing questions to supervisees from a position of curiosity about their work makes it easier for the supervisees;
3. Supervisors should be respectful, they should suspend judgment and avoid premature certainty about what is best for their supervisees;
4. Supervisors need to be respectful listeners who do not understand too quickly, if ever, what the other means;
5. Supervisors should maintain a position that is nonexpert and nonhierarchical. The effort to dissolve that hierarchy invites supervisees' input and puts the supervisor in a more facilitative role.

To date there is no research yet on the new model of *positive supervision*, however, there is some research on solution-focused supervision available. As described earlier, I composed my model of positive supervision using research and applications from traditional supervision, solution-focused supervision, and positive psychology. In this way, positive supervision applies a broader range of models than traditional or solution-focused supervision models do.

Triantafillou (1997) conducted a pilot-study on solution-focused supervision in youth health care in Canada. He found that supervisees reported more satisfaction with this form of supervision and felt more competent in comparison to other supervision models. Another finding was that their clients improved more than when the supervisees receiving traditional supervision. The author also provides suggestions for a solution-focused supervision training course.

Wei-Su (2008) did research on solution-focused supervision in Taiwan. She concluded that this model of supervision empowers supervisees: "In sum, SFS (Solution-Focused Supervision) is a model of empowerment, which can facilitate an empowered helping relationship and fully exert the behaviors and effects of empowerment." (p. 18).

> **"** Positive supervision gives me strength and pleasure. I am always amazed by the myriad of solution-focused questions and the positive approach. This supervision gives me a sense of empowerment. **"**

Positive Psychology and Solution-Focused Brief Therapy: A Comparison

Bannink and Jackson (2011) compare Positive Psychology (PP) and Solution Focus (SF). Here is a summary of their comparison.

The main similarities between PP and SF are:
- Both are part of a wave of positive approaches to change;
- In medical contexts both share a *health focus* instead of an *illness focus*;
- The focus is not to get away from what clients do not want, but towards what clients do want;
- Both investigate people's strengths and resources;
- Both share the goal of learning and promoting how individuals, families, and communities thrive;
- Both look at the past to find workable solutions and previous successes;
- Both do not seek or create pathology;
- Both do not use extensive diagnosis of problems;
- Both have as their philosophical roots a social constuctivist tradition;
- Both are still relatively unknown to each other.

The main differences between PP and SF are:
- The nature of Positive Psychology is academic, it is the scientific understanding of effective interventions to build thriving individuals,

families, and communities; the nature of SF is finding what works for this client at this moment in this context;

- PP talks of strengths: there is an interest in the constructs of 'personality'; SF has no interest or belief in universal strengths. SF picks out salient aspects of a particular situation, finding resources of exceptions within contexts;
- PP asks: where are you now and where do you want to go (from A to B); SF begins with the end in mind and works backwards (from B to A);
- PP wants to find out what is generally true and produces theories that can be tested; SF has a not-knowing stance: every case is different;
- PP's attitude is *leading* (if you are depressed try this gratitude exercise); SF's attitude is *leading from one step behind*: asking questions in order to draw out clients' expertise;
- PP's focus is mainly individual: what happens in the head; SF's focus is more interactional: the action is in the interaction. The mental is manifest in our way of action. Lately PP adopts the view that strengths are not fixed traits across settings and time, therefore the view of PP and SF about strengths might begin to converge.

Bannink and Jackson conclude that both fields could benefit from each other: SF from the PP research and practice and PP from the SF research and using *SF language*. SF may be more art than science and PP more science than art but they overlap fruitfully in any practical quest for human flourishing.

As an example of 'action in interaction' take a look at the flight of geese. As each goose flaps its wings it creates uplift for the bird following. By flying in a V-formation the whole flock has 71% greater flying range than if the bird flew alone.

Whenever a goose falls out of formation, it suddenly feels the drag and resistance of trying to fly alone and quickly gets back into formation to take an advantage of the lifting power of the bird immediately in front. And when the lead goose gets tired it rotates back into the formation and another goose flies at the point position. The geese in formation honk from behind to encourage those up front to keep up their speed. When a goose becomes ill, wounded or is shot down, two geese move out of the formation and follow it down to help protect it. They stay with it until it is able to fly again or dies, then they launch out together with another formation or they catch up with their flock. The resilience in this group can be found in their interaction.

Summary

- A description of positive supervision is given.
- The four pillars of positive supervision are introduced: goal formulation, finding competence, working on progress, and reflection.
- The brief history and assumptions of positive psychology and solution-focused brief therapy are described, with a short comparison of both;
- The importance of positive emotions in supervision is explained: they ensure more creativity, flexibility, and empathy and build relationships, resilience, and health;
- Four basic solution-focused questions are discussed, which serve as the backbone of this book.

Part II
Practical Applications

Chapter 3
Pillar 1: Goal Formulation

Failing to plan is planning to fail.
Mihaly Csikszentmihalyi

In this chapter you find the description of Pillar 1, the positive start and goal formulation. After a positive introduction and the building of *rapport*, supervisees are invited to share their goal for the supervision. In this chapter there is a little detour to research done on *hope theory,* originating from positive psychology (PP), which also considers the formulation of the *destination* – the goal – as important. Six applications of goal formulation follow and ten tips for supervisees are given to get the best out of their supervisors and their supervision.

Introduction and Building Rapport

The introduction usually sets the tone for further sessions. In positive supervision getting acquainted is always done in a positive way. Building a good working relationship is done by asking supervisees about their work, relationships, and hobbies. What do they like about their job? What are they good at? What hobbies do they have and what excites them about their hobbies? From the start the supervisors ask competence questions ("How exactly do you do that? How do you manage to do that so well?") and make compliments. These questions can be seen as icebreakers, but they may also be the start of uncovering useful information about strengths and solutions already present in the supervisees' life.

During the first session the supervisors provide information about themselves and also describe the course supervision follows, such as completing a supervision agreement, writing reports, supervision costs, etc. (see Chapter

9). Also the supervisors inform their supervisees about their way of supervising: using a traditional problem-focused or a positive model or perhaps a combination of both if they know how to do both. Transparency about the model the supervisors use is important, so supervisees may decide whether they think they are working with the right person. Problem-focused supervision can be combined with positive supervision or supervisees may be asked how they would like to be addressed: using the *problem-solving paradigm* or the *solution-building paradigm* (after explaining both models).

A great question to start with is asking supervisees how they learn best. For example, do they like to follow advice or to be invited to think for themselves and experiment? This choice doesn't have to be final: each session or case can be approached differently, according to the wishes of the supervisors or supervisees. The same applies to peer supervision.

Kolb published his learning styles model in 1984. His *experiential learning theory* (ELT) works on two levels: a four-stage cycle of learning and four separate learning styles. Much of Kolb's theory is concerned with the learner's cognitive processes. Kolb states that learning involves the acquisition of abstract concepts that can be applied flexibly in a range of situations. In his theory, the impetus for the development of new concepts is provided by new experiences. However, the model has come under severe criticism for its insufficient attention to the actual process of reflection itself, its lack of empirical support, its very rigid and sequential nature, and its inherent simplification of the learning process in general. Therefore, it may be a better alternative to invite the supervisees to come up with their preferred way of learning.

Hope Theory

In *hope theory* goal formulation is of great importance. Already in the 1950s doctors and psychologists were pointing to the important role of hope in health and well-being.

In his 1959 address to the American Psychiatric Association, psychiatrist Menninger suggested that the power of hope was an untapped source of strength and healing for patients. He defined hope as a *positive expectancy of goal attainment* and *an adventure, a going forward, a confident search* (p. 484). Menninger stated that hope is an indispensable factor in psychiatric treatment and in psychiatric education.

The interest in hope in psychotherapy was initially aimed at reducing despair rather than increasing hope. Given the link between despair and suicide, Beck, Weissman, Lester, and Trexles (1974) focused on reducing hopelessness. Their definition of hopelessness was: *a system of cognitive schemas whose common denomination is negative expectations about the future* (p.

864). Reducing hopelessness, however, is not the same as increasing hope. Frank (1974) described *restoration of morale*, for the first time using a positive formulation instead of a negative one.

Bakker, Bannink, and Macdonald (2010) state that a positive focus proves very useful in crisis situations. The available time usually does not lend itself to an elaborate diagnosis and, further to this, people in crisis benefit from regaining confidence in their personal competency and having a future-oriented approach. Think, for example, of questions such as: "How do you cope?" or "What has helped you in these past few weeks, even just a little bit?"

In the 1990s Snyder and his colleagues developed the *hope theory*, in which they propose a two-factor cognitive model of hope that similarly focuses on goal attainment. Not only does Snyder focus on expectancies, but also on the motivation and planning that are necessary to attain goals. He defines hope as a *positive emotional state that is based on an interactively derived sense of successful (a) agency and (b) pathways (planning to meet goals)* (Snyder, 1994).

In addition to setting goals, hope theory encourages therapists and clients to set goals that stretch the clients. In hope theory, goals that are difficult enough to be challenging, but easy enough to be accomplished, are called *stretch goals*. Such goals encourage the clients not only to repair problems, but also to grow as an individual. For example, a stretch goal might be to increase well-being or connectedness, instead of just solving the problem. Continuously setting and meeting stretch goals is a way to move oneself toward a more positive, strengths-based stance.

The above definitions tie hopeful thinking expressly to goals. By focusing on goal objects, we are able to respond effectively to our surrounding environment. Snyder, Michael, and Cheavens (1999) made the distinction between high-hope people and low-hope people. Compared to the vague and ambiguous nature of the goals for low-hope people, high-hope persons (Snyder et al., 1999) are more likely to clearly conceptualize their goals.

Hope theory states that hope can be seen as a journey. Three components are needed: a destination (goal), a road map (pathway thinking), and a means of transport (agency thinking). It is a thinking process that taps a sense of agency and pathways for one's goals. Research on athletes shows that sports performances are increased when individuals envision the sequence of steps necessary to perform well. The *pathway component* involves a person's belief that s/he can set goals and devise multiple ways to reach them. Once goals are set, a person's thoughts are focused on his or her ability to plan ways to reach these goals. When a route to a goal becomes blocked, those who are more hopeful devise alternate ways to pursue them. If a goal is permanently blocked, high hope people set a substitute goal that is satisfying. The *agency component* involves the person's conviction that s/he has the inner determination to implement his plans, even when faced with obstacles. Successful steps on the pathway towards a goal fuel a person's inner determination that, in turn, propels further progression towards the goal. To have a high hope level, a person must activate both components. *Goals* are the first component of hope. They are the mental targets of human action. Therefore, hope is something you do, not something you have or don't have.

The three components of hopeful thinking – goals, pathway thinking, and agency thinking – are so intertwined that the elicitation of any one should ignite the entire process of hopeful thought. Research also showed that optimism and hope are highly and positively correlated.

A severely ill man was in hospital. The doctors had given up any hope of recovery. They were unable to ascertain what the man was suffering from. Fortunately a doctor famous for his diagnostic skills would be visiting the hospital. The doctors said that maybe they could cure him if this famous doctor was able to diagnose him. When the doctor arrived the man was almost dead. The doctor looked at him briefly, mumbled moribundus (Latin for dying), and walked over to the next patient. A few years later the man – who did not know a word of Latin – succeeded in finding the famous doctor. "I would like to thank you for your diagnosis. The doctors had said that if you were able to diagnose me, I would get better."

The Importance of Goal Formulation

Hope theory demonstrates the importance of determining the destination, the goal.

Just as our supervisees sometimes do not ask what the goal of their clients is, supervisors sometimes do not ask what the goal of their supervisees is. And if the goal is formulated, it is sometimes the goal of the supervisor and not the goal of the supervisees (or in therapy: the goal of the therapist and not the goal of the clients).

A goal formulation question to the supervisees is: "How will you know that this supervision has been useful?" or "What do you like to have achieved by the end of this supervision?"

Bordin (1979) also mentions the importance of goal formulation in supervision. According to him, three components play a role in the creation of a good *alliance* (working relationship):

- The *goal* of supervision (what is the goal of the supervisees);
- The *task* (how would the supervisees like accomplish that);

- The *relationship* between the supervisees and supervisors (I will come back to the working relationship in Chapter 8).

Exercise 9   Goal, Task, and Alliance

Ask supervisees the above questions about the goal, task, and alliance and discuss how you could help them in the best possible way.

> From the first minute it was clear that this supervision was going to be very different. Instead of discussing a therapy by naming the problem of the client, making a holistic theory and problem-focused functional behavior analysis, in each therapy that I wanted to discuss the supervisor asked me, 'What is the goal of this therapy? What does this client want to achieve, what should it bring him or her? This sounds very straightforward, yet I noticed that this question is not always asked explicitly in my therapies. Therefore my clients and I sometimes had different goals in mind.

Research by Wiseman (2009) among five thousand people shows that successful people perform the following five things. Goal formulation is one of them.

1. They have a goal and name specific subgoals that they realize step by step;
2. They inform friends, family, and colleagues about their goals. The advantage of this is that others can help when there are obstacles on the way to the goal. Informing others about your goals also has the advantage that it generates more determination;
3. They imagine what the positive consequences are of achieving their goals;
4. They reward themselves when they have reached a subgoal and plan beforehand how they will reward themselves;
5. They record their progress as concretely as possible in a diary or on a computer, or they graph their improvements.

Sometimes, however, it is not the supervisees, but the supervisors who determine the goal of the supervision or are bound to the requirements of a training institute. In positive supervision one works as much as possible with the supervisees on the goals which motivate them. In addition, sometimes supervisors and/or supervisees are faced with requirements for which they have little or no motivation. In this case it is important for supervisors to draw on (or leverage) the alliance with their supervisees (and if necessary give acknowledgment) and to invite them to comply with those requirements (see Chapter 8) if necessary.

Take as an example the problem-focused intervention of *challenging dysfunctional beliefs* in traditional CBT. With this technique unhelpful cognitions are detected and repaired: the aim is to help clients develop more realistic cognitions by challenging unhelpful ones. From a Positive CBT perspective the approach is, rather, to find which functional cognitions are already present; these do not need to be challenged and can be repeated if the clients consider it useful (Bannink 2012b, 2013, 2014a). This eliminates the necessity to detect dysfunctional cognitions and challenge them (rather than fixing what is wrong, one is building what is right, see Chapter 1). However, problem-focused interventions such as challenging techniques can be discussed in positive supervision when the supervisees and/or supervisors consider this desirable or necessary. Since 2006 the Dutch Association for Behavioural and Cognitive Therapies (VGCt) contains the section Solution-Focused CBT. Within this section it is assumed that any CBT therapist, as well as knowing the Solution Focus (SF) approach, should also be able to use problem-focused interventions, which can either be addressed in positive supervision or in another problem-focused supervision.

The risk of failure is high when there is no agreement on the goal between supervisors and supervisees. If there is no common goal to work on or if the goal has not been formulated, evaluation of the supervision becomes difficult, if not impossible. Because how do supervisees and supervisors know when the supervision can be concluded and whether they are on the right track?

Goals are often formulated in negative terms (*avoidance goals*), for example: "I want to be less of a perfectionist"; "I want get to rid of my insecurity"; "I want to do less paperwork at home." It is, however, important to define the goal:

- in *positive terms*, so that it is explicit what the supervisees are moving toward rather than away from (*approach goals*): What do the supervisees want (to have instead of the problem)?;
- *in a process form*, because the goal is not static;
- *in the here and now*, so the supervisees can start the solution immediately;
- *as specific* as possible;
- *within the control* of the supervisees;
- *in the language* of the supervisees.

Case 5 Positive Goals

A supervisee describes a number of goals in negative terms. At the end of the supervision he would like to "be less confused" by some of his clients, with the result that he gives up his initial plans. He also wants to be "less tense" when seeing clients and to feel "less insecure," which sometimes makes him wonder whether he should continue in this profession.

The supervisor asks what he would like to have instead of these – negatively formulated and still abstract – avoidance goals. Instead of less confusion, he wants to be able to hold the focus. He also wants to feel relaxed and confident in sessions with his clients and he would like to know whether he should continue to be in this profession.

The supervisor then invites the supervisee to come up with examples of exceptions to the problem: situations in which he succeeds (or succeeded) – if only a little bit – or was able to hold the focus and feel relaxed and confident, so as to get a detailed picture of his goal. What is it exactly the supervisee does in those situations? How do others notice? What exactly does *relaxed* and *confident* look like? These examples should be as specific and detailed as possible, so the supervisor could – so to speak – make a film about it at the end of the session.

If you make a grocery list, do you put things on it you don't want to buy? If you were to do that, there are still about 5000 products that you can buy in the supermarket. Of course you will make a list of things you do want to buy. So invite your supervisees to list what they do want instead of what they don't want.

Exercise 10 Problem for You

It is common in supervision that the conversation is about clients who are not present. For example, your supervisees tell you how difficult they think a client is or that a particular intervention did not work out well. As a supervisor you may respond by, "How is this a problem *for you*?" With this question you bring the conversation back to the supervisees and their alliances with their clients. In this way it becomes easier to invite supervisees to talk about what they want to see instead of the problem and when there are exceptions to the problem they are experiencing with their clients.

When setting goals hopeful *stretch goals* (Snyder, 1994, also see above) can be established: goals that are challenging enough for the supervisees and yet not too difficult. With setting stretch goals supervisees reach further and beyond just reducing what they don't want. Other goal formulation questions also stimulate positive emotions, such as *the miracle question* (see below), the question what supervisees want to have instead of their problem or what supervisees want to have achieved at the end of the supervision. It is good to dream about the preferred future and future successes, because research shows that the visualization of this behavior, just as athletes do, activate the same areas in the brain as when actually performing this behavior (Ganis, Thompson, & Kosslyn, 2004).

> The Greek philosopher Aristotle (1998) used to say that having a goal is important. "A happy person is like a stone that falls to the ground and stays there quietly. After all, everything and everyone on earth pursues a goal, which is somewhere hidden inside of him. A stone wants to fall on the earth. Fire wants to go up into the sky. A person wants to be happy. If that person has developed his inner talents – his intellectual characteristics and traits – in the right way, then he has achieved the good life and is happy."

Designing a desired outcome calls on using your imagination. Consider *the miracle question*, where someone is invited to fantasize about the preferred future, after a miracle has happened and the problems are solved (see below). Einstein stated that imagination is more important than knowledge, because knowledge is limited to all we know and understand, while imagination embraces the entire world and all there ever will be to know and understand. Oettingen and Stephens (cited in Moskowitz & Grant, 2009) argue that the self-help industry would have us to believe that *to think positive* is the single most effective means of getting what we want. And though empirical research does consistently find that optimistic beliefs foster motivation and successful performance, recent research reveals that alternate forms of thinking positively about the future (*wishful thinking* and *indulging*) are less beneficial for effortful action, performance, and well-being. Whether a person indulges in a desired future (has positive fantasies about a desired future) or actually judges a desired future as within reach (has positive expectations about a desired future) has very different implications for effortful action and successful performance. In hope theory terms (see above) this is called *agency thinking*. Oettingen proposes a model of fantasy realization that serves to turn free fantasies about a desired future into binding goals. The model assumes that mentally contrasting aspects of the future and reality activate expectations about attaining a desired future that in turn leads to persistent goal striving and effective goal attainment in the case of high expectations.

In her *fantasy realization theory* (Oettingen, 1999; Oettingen, Hönig, & Gollwitzer, 2000) she elucidates three routes to goal setting that result from how people elaborate their fantasies about desired futures. One route leads to expectancy-based goal commitment, whereas the other two routes lead to goal commitment independent of expectations.

Mental contrasting is the expectancy-based route and rests on mentally contrasting fantasies about a desired future with aspects of the present reality. When people use the self-regulatory strategy of mental contrasting they first imagine a desired future and then reflect on the respective negative reality, emphasizing a necessity to change the present reality to achieve the desired future. This necessity to act should activate relevant expectations of success, which then informs goal commitment. When engaging in mental contrasting individuals first elaborate a desired future, establishing the positive future as their reference point and only thereafter elaborate aspects of the present reality, thereby perceiving the negative aspects as obstacles standing in the way of attaining the future. Reversing this order (i.e., reverse mental contrasting) by first elaborating the negative reality followed by elaboration of the desired future, thwarts construal of the present standing in the way of the future and thus fails to elicit goal commitment congruent with expectations of success (Oettingen, Pak, & Schnetter, 2001). This finding is important, because based on this research one should first consider where you want to end (B) and then return to the present situation (A), not the other way around as is the case in problem-focused conversations. This is referred to as *from B to A management,* instead of traditional *from A to B management* (Bannink, 2010a).

The second route, *indulging,* consists solely of fantasizing about a positive future. There are no reflections on the present reality that would point to the fact that the positive future is not yet realized. A necessity to act is not induced and expectations of success are not activated and used.

The third route, *dwelling,* consists of merely reflecting on the negative reality, producing continual ruminations, as no fantasies about a positive future designate the direction to act. A necessity to act is not included and expectations are not activated and used.

Numerous studies show that mental contrasting turns free fantasies into binding goals by activating expectations, thus influencing subsequent goal commitment and goal-directed behavior. Mental contrasting enables people to commit to their desired future and is effective in promoting commitment to goals that are initially hard to commit to. It can be used as a *metacognitive strategy* to help people manage and improve their everyday lives. "Making fantasies come true is not merely the stuff of daydreams or fairy tales. To make our fantasies come true, a person needs the appropriate thought processes to activate expectations and commitment" (Oettingen & Stephens, 2009, p. 174).

Exercise 11 **If-Then Training**
Gollwitzer (1999) found that people can delegate the initiation of goal-directed behavior to environmental stimuli by forming *implementation intentions* (*if-then plans* of the format: "If situation X is encountered, then I will perform behavior Y"). Forming implementation intentions facilitates detecting, attending to, and recalling the critical situation. Moreover, in the presence of the critical situation the initiation of the specified goal-directed behavior is immediate, efficient and does not need a conscious intent. Supervisees who want to change their behavior are invited to participate in an if-then training, based on mental contrasting (see above). They write down three if-then assumptions: 1. One to *overcome an obstacle*: if I feel exhausted after work, then I will put on my running shoes and go for a jog in the neighborhood; 2. One to *prevent the obstacle*: if I hear the clock chime five, then I will pack my things and leave the office to go for a run; 3. One to *identify a good opportunity to act*: if the sun is shining, then I will go for a 30-minute jog in the park).

Goal-formulation is important throughout the entire supervision process, but may also apply to every session. Useful questions are:

- What do you want to have achieved at the end of this supervision (or this session) to be satisfied?
- How will you know that you have got what you want out of this supervision?
- How will I, as your supervisor, know that the supervision is useful for you?
- How do you learn best and how can I best help you?
- How can I be most useful to you?
- How will you let me know that the supervision is on the right track?
- How will I, as your supervisor, know that you are on the right track?
- Suppose it is three months from now, how else will you know that this supervision has been useful?
- How has previous supervision been useful to you?
- How will you let me know that I have to do something different?
- What should I know about your way of working?
- How will you know you are making progress in your work?

When in supervision a case of a client is being presented, start by asking about the goal: "What will be the best result for you in presenting this case?" or "How will you know presenting this case has been useful?" The same applies for listening to or viewing audio- or videotapes. If the goal of listening to or viewing the tape is overlooked, the discussion may be about what went wrong or turned out to be fine, and this may not be the best result (goal) for the supervisee. The same applies to establishing the agenda: it is useful to first establish the goal for every issue on the agenda (see Chapter 9).

In summary, inviting supervisees to design their goal, their preferred future, is an important first step. It is useful if this fantasy about the future is then is compared with the current situation in order to overcome possible obstacles in the present to get closer to the goal. This is the same sequence as in solution-focused brief therapy (SFBT): start at B (goal), check how closely the goal has been approached at this moment (A: where are you now and what works in getting there?), and how further progress looks like (and how to overcome possible obstacles).

> ❝ I was given the opportunity to experience how positive supervision works. And how well it works! This supervision not only offered me a very nice addition in working with my clients, but also helped me in my own development as a psychotherapist. First and foremost it was helpful in formulating a clear goal: what is it I wanted to achieve? In addition it was helpful by not only shedding light on competencies I don't (yet) possess, but also by especially highlighting competencies which show that the desired development is already under way, as well as revealing which competencies I want to strengthen further. ❞

Participants in a study done by King (2001) were asked to write down their ideal future, in which all had gone well and they had met their hopes and goals, for a few minutes on four consecutive days (Best possible self). One of the control groups was asked to write about a traumatic event that had happened to them for those minutes on four consecutive days. Another control group was asked to write about life goals as well as a trauma for the four days. Another control group was asked to write about their plans for the day on those four days.

The results were that the future-oriented group reported more subjective well-being after the experiment than the controls. The trauma and the future-oriented group both had less illness when followed up five months later.

Therefore, invite your supervisees to write about their life in ten years time, when everything is going well and they are successful in their work and life. Then invite them to distill a goal or mission they can work on every day. Or invite them to make a ten-year plan to ensure their mission will work out fine.

Exercise 12 Opening Question

Think about what *opening question* you usually start a supervision session with. You may opt for a problem-focused question: "What are the problems you want to discuss today?" or "What needs to change?" You may opt for a question that implies that you will work hard: "What can I do for you today?" Or you may choose a question about the goal of the supervisee: "What is the goal of this session?" or "What would you like to have accomplished by the end of this supervision (or this session) so you can say it has been useful to see me?" and: "What would tell you this supervision was a success?" Or do you ask: "What are your best hopes from this supervision?" and "What difference will that make?"

The opening question determines in part the answers you receive. Try out all the possibilities and note the differences in your supervisees' reactions and in the atmosphere of the sessions.

❝ My supervisor taught me the power of an optimistic, realistic, and hopeful approach. Positive supervision invited me to reflect on what I want to achieve and how I can rely on my own competencies and strengths. I was encouraged to explore what I had already achieved in working with my clients, what works, what I want to continue doing, and what I would like to do differently. ❞

Six Applications for Goal Formulation

Below six applications for useful goal-formulation are described.

1. Compare Yourself With a Taxi Driver

Sometimes I compare myself as a supervisor with a taxi driver. I tell my supervisees: "Just suppose I am a taxi driver and you are the customer. When you get in my car – after a friendly greeting – my first question will be: 'Where do you want to go?" (and not: "Where do you want to get away from?" or "Where are you from?"). My first question is about the destination (the goal) of the supervisees.

If a customer gets in my taxi and says he doesn't know the destination, I will not just start driving, because the probability that the client will arrive at his destination is extremely small. I will ask further questions to find out what the destination may be or how the customer can get a clearer picture of his destination. If the customer says that he doesn't want go to the airport (e.g., "I don't want to procrastinate") I will ask questions about *where he does want to go*. It is my expertise and responsibility as a taxi driver to bring the customer as safe and comfortable as possible (this is called *the least burden principle*), and take the shortest route to his destination. Only then is everyone happy when the customer gets out of my cab (Bannink & McCarthy, 2014).

2. Use the Four Basic Solution-Focused Questions

In goal-formulation questions 1 and 2 of the four basic solution-focused questions are used, as described in Chapter 2. The first question is about the best hopes of the supervisees. As stated earlier hope plays an important role in the success of psychotherapy and probably of supervision. Hope is by definition future-oriented: you cannot hope for anything in the past or present. The question is not *whether* the supervisees have best hopes, but *what* their best hopes are. Then the supervisor asks: "What else you are hoping for? And what else?"

The supervisor continues asking, "What else?" until the supervisees indicate "that's pretty much it." With these questions about the supervisees' hopes the supervisor gets a good impression of the – often many or even all – *roads to Rome*. Rome itself comes into view when Question 2 is answered, "What difference will that make? What else will be different (for yourself, your clients, your colleagues, etc.)?" In answering that question the supervisees come up with a detailed description of their preferred future.

It is important to make a distinction between the ways to Rome and Rome itself (in other words the means or subgoals and the goal/destination). The goal is the desired situation in the future; the means are the roads to Rome. Just as clients in psychotherapy do, supervisees often first formulate the means when asked about their goal. If the supervisor (or colleagues in peer supervision) accepts a means as being the goal, the preferred future of the supervisees often is not well formulated and it remains unclear when the supervision is considered useful and meaningful. Means are, for example: "getting more assertive with my clients," "dealing better with clients who are angry," or "procrastinating less when paperwork is involved." In this case the goal will become clearer when the supervisor asks: "Suppose in a few months you will be as assertive as you want to be, what difference will that make in your work? What will be different and what will you be doing differently?" If one or more roads to Rome turn out to be blocked, then Rome may be reached by using other routes, so there is no need for stagnation. Compare this with the above-mentioned research about high-hope people, who are better at designing alternative solutions and are still able to achieve their goal, even if the original route is blocked. They also anticipate better on possible obstacles, which increases their resilience compared to low-hope people.

Case 6   **Means and Ends**

A supervisee is asked about his goal in supervision. He mentions that he wants to have more theoretical background in his work. Sometimes he thinks that he is just doing things in therapy without knowing why. The supervisor realizes that this is a means (road to Rome, the means) and not the goal (Rome itself, the end). When asked what difference this will make for him, the supervisee looks surprised: he has never thought about this before. The same applies to the next questions about what difference it will make for his clients and his colleagues. An alternative question about differences is that the supervisor asks him what it will *mean* for him (and others) when he has more theoretical background. The supervisee is invited – as homework – to reflect on that question, so in the next meeting he can tell what the differences are.

3. Follow the Protocol for the First Session With Goal Formulation

All questions are submitted to all supervisees present (see Appendix 2).
- *Problem* (this part may also be skipped): "What brings you here? How is this a problem for you? What have you already tried that has been useful?"
- *Goal formulation*: "What would you like to have achieved at the end of the supervision (or this session)?" Here one may ask the *miracle question* or another questions about goal formulation.
- *Exceptions:* "When have you caught a glimpse of your goal (or the miracle)? How did you do that? How did you make that happen?" Alternatively, "When are there moments that the problem is absent or less noticeable? How did you make that happen?"
- *Scaling* of:
  - *Progress* since the appointment for the first session was made: Where are you today on a scale of 10–0? How did you reach that point on the scale already? How did you do that?
  - *Motivation*: 10 means you're willing to give it your all, and 0 means you're not willing to put in any effort.
  - *Confidence* that the goal can be reached: 10 means that you are very confident, and 0 means you have no confidence at all that your goal can be reached.

- *Task or homework suggestions*: behavioral tasks, observational tasks, or no task (see Chapter 8 and 9).
- The question, "Do you think it will be useful for you to come back?" If so: "When would you like to come back?"
- Use of the *Session Rating Scale* (SRS), see Chapter 6 and Appendix 6.

4. Use Other Questions About Goal Formulation

Other questions for goal-formulation can be found below. Bannink (2010b, 2013) described 1001 questions, including many ones about goal formulation.

- What is the purpose of your visit?
- What do you want to have achieved the end of this supervision to be able to say that it is a success (or meaningful or useful)?
- What will be better (or different) after the supervision has ended?
- How you will notice that your goal has been achieved?
- How will others (clients, colleagues, family) notice that you have achieved your goal?
- What will be the best outcome from this supervision for you?
- What do you want to be different as a result of this supervision?
- How will you know that you have had enough supervision?
- What will make this supervision worthwhile for you?
- What would your best colleague or your clients say is your goal for supervision?
- When you picture yourself five or ten years from now, what will you say, looking back, that your goal was when you first came here?
- When will you consider your supervision to be successful?
- Suppose I am a fly on the wall at your work and I watch you working after this supervision. What will I see you do differently or better than you do now?
- How would you like to see yourself when you are at your best at work?
- If you could look into a crystal ball, what improvements do you see when your goal is reached?

Exercise 13   Variety of Questions

Goal formulation is important in supervision. Therefore, ask questions about goal-formulation at the start and possibly also at the beginning of each session or any issue on the agenda (see Chapter 9). It is convenient to know a variety of questions about goal formulation because supervisees may not always answer the question right away.

5. Ask the Miracle Question

Another way to investigate the preferred future is asking the *miracle question*: "Suppose tonight while you are asleep a miracle happens. But because you are asleep, you do not know this is happening. The miracle is that you have reached your goal in its entirety. What will be the first thing you notice tomorrow morning as you wake up that tells you this miracle has happened? What will be different? What will you be doing differently? What else? How will the rest of the day be different? How will people around you (family, colleagues, clients, friends) notice that the miracle happened? How will they react differently? And how will you then react differently?"

6. Make a Drawing or Collage

A creative way to discover what supervisees want to have (instead of problems), is making a drawing or collage. This can be done in a variety of ways. They can make two drawings: one of the preferred future and one of the current problem. They then imagine how they build a road or bridge from one drawing to the other. The steps, which can be made to reach their goal, may also be drawn in several different drawings. In this way they create a solution-focused comic strip with, for example, six drawings. The sequence in which the six drawings are made is important. Invite them to start at the last, sixth drawing: the preferred future, in which the goal is reached. The next, first one is a drawing of the current (problematic) situation. In the intermediate pictures the steps may be drawn as how to arrive at the desired situation in the sixth drawing.

Another creative way is to invite supervisees to make a collage of the situation where they, for example, want to be in one or two years from now (i.e., at the end of the supervision). The collage is made by cutting pictures and/or words from magazines and pasting these on paper. Many supervisees enjoy doing this as a homework assignment at the start of the supervision. They often hang the collage in their office to remind them of their preferred future.

Tips for Supervisees

Sometimes supervisees may require some guidance in optimizing their supervision. They should not passively wait and see what the supervisor does. Supervisees can play an active role in optimizing their supervision. I often say to my supervisees, "This is your party!" Here are ten tips for supervisees to get the best out of their supervisors and their supervision:

1. Determine the goal of the supervision: what will be the best result for you?

2. Imagine a picture of how a successful working relationship with your supervisor will look like. How will you know that the supervision is a success for both of you?
3. Start positive. Get to know each other and agree upon how you want to work together;
4. Build on your working relationship with respect and trust. Be on time, keep your promises, and follow the advice given;
5. Prepare the sessions. Make reports and plan beforehand what you want to discuss and what your goal in discussing this is;
6. Be open to new ideas, even if the ideas of your supervisor may sometimes differ from yours;
7. Ask your supervisor to introduce you to people in his or her network;
8. Occasionally show that you are grateful that your supervisor shares his or her knowledge and expertise with you;
9. Give something in return from your own knowledge and expertise, so that your supervisor may profit from it;
10. Support your supervisor by sharing things that he or she considers useful or may find interesting.

In Chapter 8 I describe tips for supervisors and supervisees in the event of disagreements or conflicts.

Top performers don't focus on pathology, but focus on their goals instead. How do they set goals? Barrell, a performance improvement expert working with famous baseball players in the USA, stated that there are "toward goals" and "away goals." Which one you use has quite an impact on performance. Toward goals have you visualize and create connections around where you are going. You are creating new connections in your brain. What is interesting is that you start to feel good at lower levels with toward goals. There are benefits earlier. Away goals have you visualize what can go wrong, which reactivates the negative emotions involved.

Source: Barrell and Ryback (2008)

More information about approach and avoidance goals and about approach and avoidance motivation is described in Bannink (2012b).

Summary

- The introduction and building of rapport takes place in a positive way, which immediately sets the tone for the rest of the supervision;
- Hope theory (based on research in PP) is outlined with the destination (goal), pathway thinking (mental roadmap), and agency thinking (motivation to take action);
- The importance of goal formulation is substantiated by the *fantasy realization theory.*
- There are three routes to goal setting that result from how people elaborate their fantasies about desired futures, of which only *mental contrasting* turns free fantasies about a desired future into binding goals;
- Six practical applications of goal formulation are presented;
- Supervisees can and should play an active role in their supervision;
- Ten tips for supervisees to get the best out of their supervisors and their supervision are given.

Chapter 4
Pillar 2: Finding Competence

Psychotherapy as defined now is where you go to talk about your troubles and your weaknesses: perhaps in the future it will also be where you go to build your strengths
Martin Seligman

This chapter describes Pillar 2: finding competence. "What is working?"is the third of the four basic solution-focused questions described in Chapter 2. Finding competence focuses on already existing abilities and on exceptions to the problem.

When asked, no supervisee ever indicates to be at 0 on a scale of 10–0, where 10 means that their goal is completely achieved and 0 means the opposite. "What is working and how did you do that?" With these questions supervisees are invited to tell you about the *road already traveled* with its acquired skills and successes, with the additional benefit of increasing positive emotions and intrinsic motivation.

This is different from most traditional supervision models, in which supervisors focus on capacities that supervisees should possess at the end of the supervision: there is attention only for the *road still to be traveled.* How this difference affects the motivation of the supervisees can be found in the story about the car wash later in this chapter. Furthermore, supervisors or their training institutions, not the supervisees themselves, often determine these competencies. This chapter discusses how to find competencies with the help of the Values in Action (VIA) *Survey of Character Strengths*, asking *competence questions*, finding exceptions (to the problem), and nineteen other applications.

> "My own experiences and my role during therapy are of course also focused on in supervision. The question: 'What is your role in the success of your client, what did you do to make this therapy successful? helps me to understand my therapeutic skills, to enhance my self-efficacy as a therapist, and to be enthusiastic in the work I am doing."

Case 7   Discuss Successes

In the Introduction I mentioned research in monkeys, showing that they learn more from their successes than from their failures. According to the biologists who did this research, this finding is probably also true for human beings. This is why I often invite my supervisees to share their (recent) successes. It is my experience that supervisees like to tell positive stories about what they have done well. Recently a supervisee told me about a successful psychotherapy with a woman, whose only son had commit suicide. The woman saw no meaning in life and was severely depressed. The supervisee had helped her by, among others things, listening to her story and by normalizing her feelings. The supervisee also explained about mourning tasks and discussed with her the possibility of a farewell letter to her son, encouraging her to look at photos of him and prepare a farewell ritual. As a result of this the client improved. When asked what the supervisee was most proud of, he said that he had been flexible in his approach and had listened to what could be helpful for this client and her needs. Of course I complimented the supervisee for everything he did that worked.

Finding Competencies

A nice way to discover (your) personal qualities or competencies (these categories are used synonymously) is taking the VIA Survey of Character Strengths. This classification of 24 *character strengths* was designed by Seligman (2002) and Peterson (2006) and was drawn up as a counterpart to the classification system of psychiatric disorders DSM-5. The survey can be found on: www.authentichappiness.org. The 24 character strengths are divided into six virtues, described in Table 3.

Table 3. Organization of the 6 virtues and 24 character strengths

---

1. Wisdom and knowledge

These are the five strengths that involve the acquisition and use of knowledge: creativity, curiosity, open-mindedness, love of learning, perspective and wisdom

2. Courage

These are the four strengths that allow one to accomplish goals in the face of opposition: bravery, persistence, integrity, and vitality

3. Humanity

These are the three strengths of tending and befriending others: love, kindness, and social intelligence

4. Justice

These are the three strengths that build a healthy community: social responsibility and loyalty, fairness, and leadership

5. Temperance

These are the four strengths that protect against excess: forgiveness and mercy, humility, prudence, self-regulation and self-control

6. Transcendence

These are the five strengths that forge connections to the larger universe and provide meaning: appreciation of beauty, gratitude, hope, humor and playfulness, and spirituality.

Exercise 14   Well-Being and Flow

Everyone has certain strengths. You go into flow when your greatest strengths are deployed to meet the challenges that come your way. Deploying your greatest strengths leads to more positive emotions, more meaning, more accomplishment, and better relationships. The top-5 qualities for well-being consist of: hope, vitality, gratitude, curiosity, and love. Invite supervisees to come up with their own strengths and qualities and ask them to make their personal Top 5 or ask them to take the VIA survey online. Then invite them to share how they already use these strengths in their work and life. Research shows that well-being increases when people use their top-5 strengths more often or in a new area in their lives. The chances of experiencing flow will also increase (Bannink, 2009a).

❝ I feel strong when I think of my answer to the miracle question, when I describe exceptions to the problem, when I reflect on where I am on the scale from 10–0 and which steps I can take to move me to a higher point on the scale. I feel competent and the urge to do more of it is great. Suddenly I realized I had more competencies as a therapist than I previously thought I had. By experiencing what positive supervision does to you, I became instantly excited to also use this approach in the treatments with my clients. **"**

Another way to find competences is to ask *competence questions*. There are three important competence questions to invite supervisees to relate their success stories:

1. How did you do that?
2. How did you decide to do that?
3. How did you manage to do that?

The first question departs from the assumption that the supervisee has done something and therefore supposes action, competence, and responsibility. The second question departs from the assumption that the supervisee has taken an active decision, affording him the opportunity to write a new life story, with influence on his or her own future. The third question invites the supervisee to relate his or her successes.

In our Western culture it may be difficult to talk about one's own successes and competence. Others may think you are an irritating brag. One has to be modest, just be normal. Therefore we often see our competencies as being nothing special. In spite of this, search with your supervisees for those things that make them proud and satisfied. You may want to ask about:

- their appearance: What do they like about themselves?
- relationships: What are they good at, what do they like about being with others?
- personality: When are they happy, kind, honest etc?
- work or school: What are they best at, what do they like about it?
- daily life: What is going well, what are they good at?

Exercise 15 Proof of Competence

Ask your supervisees what they see at the best way for you as their supervisor to collect proof of their competence. What should you, as their supervisor, pay attention to? What, according to them, can you do to achieve this? How would they like to receive your feedback?

" When your competencies are highlighted, you become a bit
bigger: you grow, breathing becomes easier, your self-efficacy
increases, and the issues you first were not sure about become
smaller and less problematic. This also has an effect on your work:
you have the courage to apply new techniques and make the
impression to your clients you are confident and skilled in helping
to solve their problems. And this is precisely the purpose of the
supervision. "

Case 8 The Road Already Traveled

The question "What works (already)?" invites supervisees to investigate how far they are on the way to their goal, rather than only looking at how far they still have to go. As an example a coaching supervisee tells that she feels already somewhat competent in her profession because she already has four years of working experience, she attended training courses and feels more relaxed within her team than at the start. Moreover, her heavy workload is easier to carry and she manages more often to reduce the number of coaching sessions. She also receives compliments from colleagues about how she operates within her team.

On a scale where 10 means that her goal is completely reached and 0 the opposite, she estimates being on a 4. She aims to be on a 6.5 at the end of the supervision and to arrive finally (in a few years time) at an 8.

This story shows the importance of focusing on the road already traveled. A local car wash ran a promotion featuring loyalty cards. Every time customers bought a car wash, they got a stamp, and a free wash when they filled up their cards with eight stamps. Other customers got a different loyalty card. They needed to collect ten stamps (rather than eight) to get a free car wash – but they were given a head start: Two stamps had already been added.

The goal was the same: buy eight additional car washes, get a reward. But the psychology was different: in one case, you're 20% of the way toward the goal; in the other case you're starting from scratch. A few months later 19% of the eight-stamp customers had earned a free wash, versus 34% of the head-start group (and the head-start group earned the free wash faster). People find it more motivating to be partly finished with a longer journey than to be at the starting gate of a shorter one. To motivate action is to make people feel as though they're closer to the finish line than they might have thought.

Goldstein, Martin, and Cialdini (2007, p. 159), who conducted this experiment, state: "When soliciting another person for help with anything, you should try to point out how that person has already taken steps towards the completion of that task."

Source: Heath and Heath (2010)

Giving compliments is a form of positive reinforcement of what works. There are four types of compliments:

1. A *direct compliment* is a positive evaluation or reaction by the supervisors in response to the supervisees. It can be about something the supervisees have said, done, or made, or about their appearance.
2. A compliment can also be about the supervisees' *personality*: "You seem to be a really caring person ... I am correct?" or "You must be a very determined person, please tell me more about this determination of yours."
3. The most beautiful compliments are the *indirect compliments*, based on a question that implies something positive about the supervisees. One way to indirectly compliment is to ask for more information about a desired outcome stated by the supervisees. These questions invite the supervisees to tell a success story about themselves: "How did you do this?"; "How were you able to ...?"; "Where did you get this great idea?" Indirect complimenting is preferable to direct complimenting because its questioning format leads supervisees to discover and state their own strengths and resources. Many supervisees accept compliments easily. Others, however, downplay or even reject them. But remember that the first goal in giving compliments is for supervisees to notice their positive changes, strengths, and resources. It is not necessary for them to openly accept the compliments.
4. *Finding exceptions*, moments where the problem is absent or less, or moments that already look a bit like the preferred future, is another way of complimenting supervisees. They apparently did something that worked. By focusing on successes the attention of the supervisees can be directed towards their strengths and possibilities instead of their weaknesses and impossibilities.

When giving direct compliments it matters how they are presented. Research by Grant Halvorson (2010) shows that children who are praised for their performance (often girls) eventually do worse than children who are praised for their efforts (often boys). Her research showed that those children who see their goals as *getting better* experience their curriculum more as fun and more interesting and absorb the instruction more deeply. They are more motivated, persevere longer when the going gets tough and the chance is greater that they are indeed better in the long run than children who are praised for their performance. Research among students report similar results. Therefore it is preferable to give supervisees direct compliments on their efforts to become better at certain skills than on how well they perform, and provide them with many indirect compliments by asking competence questions.

Exercise 16 Asking Questions About Competence

Make sure supervisees get more compliments about their efforts than about their performance. First and foremost ask questions which elicit competence, because in this way you invite them to tell success stories about themselves. They grow from telling these stories. In addition, these kinds of compliments are often more easily accepted, in contrast to direct compliments.

Exercise 17 Three Compliments

In the next supervision sessions that last longer than 5 minutes, give at least three compliments to those present and notice how the atmosphere of the conversations changes. Use a variety of the four types of compliments: direct, indirect, exceptions, and personality.

Case 9 **Coexpert**

A supervisee tells that she got confused during the last session with a client, because she didn't understand what the client, who made a rather chaotic impression, had said. What should she do or what should she have done? A problem-focused supervisor might perhaps, based on his expertise, suggest that the client is psychotic and might give the advice of referring the client to a psychiatrist for additional diagnostics. The positive-focused supervisor views the supervisee as a coexpert and asks about her expertise: Has she ever been confused before in sessions with her clients and if so what did she do then? The supervisee acknowledges she has had this feeling before and in those instances consulted her team leader as to what she should do. This eventually also resulted in a reference to the psychiatrist. The difference is that the supervisee is considered a coexpert who already knows the solution – perhaps yet unnoticed.

Not all supervisees can name their strengths. Often they are very strict with themselves and set high standards, forcing themselves to look at what they could have or should have done better. Their *self-compassion* is rather low. Self-compassion means that you can look at yourself in a friendly instead of a critical way. Buddha said: "You, yourself, as much as anyone else in the entire universe, deserves your love."

For most people having compassion for others is quite easy, but having self-compassion is often more difficult. Often misunderstood as self-indulgent, self-compassion, as defined by Neff (2011) has three aspects: (1) mindfulness of one's own thoughts and feelings, (2) a sense of a common humanity, and (3) treating oneself kindly. While building self-esteem has been linked to a number of mental health problems, including narcissism and emotional fragility, self-compassion is associated with positive effects such as satisfaction with one's own life, wisdom, optimism, curiosity, goal setting, social connectedness, personal responsibility, and emotional resilience.

Gilbert (2010) also pointed to the importance of self-compassion, not in the least for people working in the helping professions. He refers to a number of exercises from positive psychology (PP), such as *loving-kindness exercises* (mindfulness: Fredrickson, 2009) and *You at your best* (see below).

Exercise 18 Self-Compassion

Invite supervisees to answer the following three questions:
1. Find five to ten things you like about yourself;
2. Find five to ten things you do that add value to the world around you;
3. What is your proudest achievement in your work in the last twelve months?

If supervisees cannot find any strengths or resources, you may invite them to look at themselves through a more positive lens:

- What would your best friend(s) say that your strengths and resources are?
- What qualities and competences do they know you have?
- What would your kids/parents/colleagues say that your strengths and resources are?
- Where do you get the courage to change if you wish to?
- How can you make change easier for yourself?
- Where do you get your good ideas?
- How do you manage to be so determined?
- When was your last success and what did you do to make that happen?
- If you go back in time: when did you become aware that you had those strengths and qualities?
- When were others aware that you had those qualities?
- How can you use these qualities and competencies again now?
- How will others notice that you use these qualities in this situation?
- What things are easy for you to do, while others may find them difficult?
- What was easy for you when you were a child?

- If ... (e.g., a deceased person) could see how you are doing now, what will s/he be proud of?
- What would that person say about you, if that were possible?
- What would s/he say about how you have achieved this?
- How does change in your life usually take place?
- What's going well in your life, even just a little bit?
- What are you satisfied with in your life and want to keep it as it is?

Case 10 **Left and Right**

A supervisee finds it very difficult to name something she is good at or pleased about. She cannot come up with anything positive about herself. The supervisor invites her to make a list of all the points she dislikes about herself or is not happy about. These points are listed on the left side of a sheet of paper after the supervisor has drawn a vertical line in the middle of the paper. The supervisor then asks the supervisee what she would like to see instead of each point on the left side and when there are or were (small) exceptions to the problem. These are written on the right side of the paper. Then the supervisor cuts the paper in half and the left side is thrown into the wastepaper basket, which was the supervisee's idea. From then onwards, the supervisor and supervisee work only with her goals and what works for her, building solutions instead of solving problems.

> ❝Because of the positive focus the atmosphere in supervision is more relaxed. Your qualities are positively reinforced and successes are highlighted. You leave the supervision with a positive feeling and a stronger self-efficacy. Anxiety and uncertainty change into enthusiasm and confidence, which ensures you reach the desired future earlier, which is to be a competent professional.❞

De Jong and Berg (2002) emphasize that the most important task for the supervisor is to invite their supervisees to learn to listen to the ideas of their clients about how they can be useful to them. Already in Chapter 1 I suggested that the perspective of clients is most important in supervision and not the perspective of the supervisees themselves. Therefore, questions especially need to be about this perspective of the clients, such as:

- What would *your clients* say about what you do well in your cooperation with them?
- What would *your clients* say that they appreciate about you?
- What three strengths would *your clients* say you have?

Exercise 19 Which Strengths Did We Already Notice?

Invite supervisees to give a colleague who just presented a case as many compliments as possible by asking them: "What strengths did we already notice about him or her during their presentation?"

Exercise 20 Your Three Signature Strengths

In your work as a supervisor you also use your own strengths. Identify which three signature strengths have brought to where you are now in your profession. Discuss this with a colleague and ask which three strengths he or she would identify in you. Then invite your colleague to do the same: which three strengths have brought him or her this far? Also think about how you could apply your strengths even more in your work than you already do.

Another way to put the same questions, this time from the perspective of your supervisees, would be to ask: what three signature strengths would my supervisees say I/ you have?

Finding Exceptions

Another way of finding competencies is to search for exceptions to the problem. Because every problem fluctuates, there are always moments when the problem is less severe or even absent (for a while). In positive supervision the focus is especially on those moments and how that has been achieved. The focus is also on those moments when one succeeds (better) in coping with the problem. Often only small changes are needed. Once supervisees are encouraged to notice small changes – exceptions in the past or present – and validate those changes, they start noticing their own competence, start expecting other changes to happen and believing in the snowball effect of small changes. Often they already possess the beginning of solutions without knowing it. These are the exceptions to the problem (their *hidden successes*). Exception-finding questions provide clues about what else could happen; so do questions about hypothetical solutions such as: "Suppose a miracle happened and your problems are gone' or "Suppose you are a point higher on the scale." Questions about what they would like to see different in their lives and work, provide clues as to the direction in which solutions can be found. Because supervisees are considered as coexperts and are able to find solutions themselves, these solutions are a good fit, are quickly found and are permanent.

Wittgenstein (1968) stated the following about exceptions: they lie on the surface; you don't have to dig for them. But one often tends to overlook them, because one only focuses on the problem (the problem is *always* there). And even if one notices exceptions, you'll often hear that these exceptions don't count: they are not yet considered to be "a difference that makes a difference." For supervisees the problem is seen as primary (and the exceptions, if seen at all, are seen as secondary), while for the supervisor the exceptions are seen as primary. Interventions are meant to help supervisees make a similar inversion, which will lead to the development of a solution (de Shazer, 1991).

There are more curious misperceptions. Dijksterhuis (2007) states that when you pay attention to something, you tend to miss other things. In a now famous experiment about this so called inattentional blindness subjects watched a video recording of a basketball game between two teams of three players. They were instructed to choose one of the teams and count how often each member threw the ball to their team members. At one point there appeared a man dressed up as a gorilla, walking slowly through the scene. Afterwards the subjects were interviewed about how often the players tossed the ball to each other. They were also asked if they had seen something remarkable or unexpected while watching the recording. It turned out that more than 50% of the subjects had not seen the gorilla at all!

Exception-finding questions are:
- When are/were there already little pieces of the preferred future (the goal)?
- When is/was the problem less or even absent (for a while)?
- When do/did you manage the problem better?

When positive exceptions have occurred, the supervisors may ask more questions to amplify these exceptions. If they have not yet occurred, but it is possible to formulate the goal, the supervisors may ask more about the preferred future. If this is not the case, the problem may be analyzed. It is only necessary to make an analysis of the problem if no exceptions to the problem can be found and no goal can be formulated in behavioral terms ("What will you be doing differently when the problem is solved?"). In most cases, one can immediately begin working toward a solution without first elaborately mapping the problem (de Shazer, 1985).

When someone is having problems, it is usually because he or she is attending to the same thing over and over again. The statement: "Insanity is doing the same thing over and over again and expecting different results" is generally attributed to Einstein. Supervisees are invited to shift their attention from analysis, explanations, and problems, to descriptions, thoughts, actions, and feelings that can help them flourish. Supervisors listen for openings in problem-focused conversations. These openings can be about what supervisees would like to see different in their lives, openings about exceptions to the problem or the goal, openings about competencies and resources, openings about who and what might be helpful in taking next steps. Improvement is often realized by redirecting attention from dissatisfaction about a status quo to a positive goal and to start taking steps in the direction of that goal.

If exceptions are deliberate, supervisees can do them again. If exceptions are spontaneous, they might seek more information about them, for instance by predicting when these exceptions might occur.

> " What is more delicious and satisfying than filleting a complex problem? By doing that I sometimes forget to look for moments when the problem didn't happen or what small steps have been taken in the desired direction. "

Walter and Peller (1992) put together a map for finding exceptions and developing solutions:

- From wish or complaint to goal: What would you like to change about that?
- Are there (already) exceptions to the problem?
- If so, can they be repeated? Do more of what works.
- Are there any spontaneous exceptions? Discover more about them.
- Are there no exceptions, but can a goal be formulated? Do a (small) piece of it.

Whenever possible, the wishes and complaints are phrased as a goal, i.e., as wishes or complaints about which something can be done. The questions that are asked lead to three types of homework suggestions (see Chapter 9). If workable exceptions can be found, the miracle question (the hypothetical solution) is usually redundant.

Further exception-finding questions are:

- What is different/better since you made the appointment for supervision?
- What is better since the last supervision session?
- Which moments already look a bit like the miracle (or the preferred future) you described?
- What is different about those moments?
- What do you do differently then? How did you do that?

- How was that different for you? How was that different for others (colleagues, clients, etc)?
- What would those people who know you well say about how you succeeded in doing that?
- How big is the chance that you could do that again?
- When was the last time you had a great working day?
- When is the problem less or even absent (for a while)?
- What do you do differently then?
- When did you not have this problem, even when you expected you would?
- What happens when the problem ends or starts to end?
- How come the problem is not worse?
- Suppose you could remember an exception, which one would that be?
- When did you succeed in handling the problem (a bit) better?
- Which aspects of your life and work would you like to keep the way they are?

Exercise 21 Keep It the Way It Is

Invite supervisees to keep a diary for a week (or longer if they wish) to examine things they don't want to change. Ask them to pay attention to the things in their life that *they would like to keep the way they are* and write them down. Ask them to pay themselves a compliment at the end of every day based on their diary and write it down.

Case 11 Finding Exceptions

A supervisee complains that in the sessions with her clients she often runs out of time, which leads to a lack of time in the following sessions. This produces a great deal of stress and, therefore, she thinks she is not a good professional. Because there are always exceptions the supervisor asks, "When do you succeed (and have you succeeded) in staying within the time-limit?"; "How do/did you do that?" After a little thought the supervisee describes some examples of when, in the past, she is able to stay within the time limits. Strategies she found effective are: telling the client at the beginning of the session that she wants to improve in time management, which means that she will be more strict in living by the clock; a kitchen timer on the table that goes off 5 minutes before time; and if the meeting comes to completion on time, not elaborating on new issues that clients might bring forward. The supervisor compliments her on these effective strategies and asks her where she is on the scale of 10–0, where 10 means that she completes all sessions on time and 0 means the opposite. She estimates being at a four and would like to get to eight. The supervisor asks, "Does she think doing a homework task might be useful?" The supervisee agrees to the suggestion to observe those moments in which she succeeds in stopping, even a bit better, on time, thus being slightly higher on the scale than four, and to monitor what she is doing differently then.

Exercise 22 Do More of What Works

Invite supervisees to answer these two questions. Less supervision may be necessary than was initially expected.
How can I go on with what works?
How can I do more of what works?

Nineteen Ways to Find Competence

Here are nineteen more ways in which to find competence. All suggestions/examples can be used both by supervisors and supervisees.

1. Ask About Competence Transference

A nice way to find competencies is to look for qualities and skills in other areas in life. What interests your supervisees? What are they good at? And how can they transfer those strengths and skills to bring them closer to their goal?

Lamarre and Gregoire (1999) describe a technique called *competence transference* in which they invite clients to talk about other areas of competence in their lives, such as sports or a hobby or a special talent. They then ask clients to bring those abilities to bear in order to reach their goals. For instance, they described how a client suffering from a panic disorder learned to relax by applying his knowledge of deep-sea diving whenever he experienced anxiety.

Case 12 Competence Transference

A supervisee told me how she sometimes became discouraged because so little progress was made during her conflict management sessions. When asked at the start of the supervision, she told me about one of her hobbies, which was horse riding. After her comment about discouragement, I remembered her hobby and asked what made horse riding so special for her. She answered with a smile: "I always get the most difficult horses and know what to do with them." I asked her what her colleagues knew about her strengths and competence to let her work with these horses. "Because I have a lot of patience with them," she explained. "And what else?" She said: "Because even if a horse has been disobedient that particular day, before I leave I always hug the horse and say: "Tomorrow will be a better day."
I invited her to think about how she might use her horse-riding skills in her conflict management sessions (even more than she already did). After some practice she told me that it worked: she became less discouraged and succeeded more often in thinking: "It will be better next time."

2. Design *Your Best Self-portrait*

You may hear something positive about yourself when you change jobs and there is a farewell speech, in which your boss tells you how delighted he was to have you as an employee and how all your colleagues are going to miss you. Or you may hear something positive for the first time about someone at his or her funeral. But this can be changed!

Invite your supervisees to ask 10–20 people in their life to give them three written stories that describe what worked when the supervisee made a contribution in some way. Ask them to collect all the stories and bring them together looking for common themes, surprises, and insights. Then ask them to synthesize all the different contributions into a *Best self-portrait*; summarize their findings or create a project based on the synthesis and share the results with important people in their life. People often combine this exercise with their VIA Survey results to get a clear picture of their character strengths in action, as well as seeing how closely the strengths they perceive they have line up with the strengths others perceive them to have.

Note that 20 people may sound like a daunting number, but think of the impact this might have. Supervisees will be having meaningful conversations with 20 people in their life; they will be soliciting positive, engaging comments from these people; they will probably be connecting with people across numerous domains of their life – personal, social, work, or spiritual. Consider how transformative this can be for them, for the others, and for these relationships.

3. Celebrate Successes

Invite supervisees to celebrate their successes by:

- Coming up with a positive statement about themselves and saying this statement out loud a few times every day. For example: "I am an open and honest person with good friends."
- Writing a positive statement about themselves and carry this statement with them wherever they go, so they can read it if it suits them. Or invite them to stick this statement on their bathroom mirror or kitchen cabinet, so they see it often. Some people may think this is a bit weird, but many say that it is helpful to look at something they find satisfying from time to time.
- Choosing three character strengths every day and find out at the end of the day when they have used these strengths and how this helped them to create positive *self-fulfilling prophecies*.

Exercise 23 Listening for Strengths

This exercise is about using your ears to hear only about the strengths a person has and nothing else. You can perform this exercise in group or peer supervision. Invite one of the supervisees to tell the others about a recent successful or pleasant event, something he or she is proud of or happy about. The others are asked to respond by giving as many compliments as possible. This includes direct compliments, competence questions, and positive statements about the personality of the supervisee (see earlier this chapter). The supervisee is then asked what compliments had the strongest impact on him or her.

Another person is then invited to tell the others about a recent nasty event, something about which he or she is ashamed, angry, or sad. The others are asked again to come up with as many compliments as possible. Then the person is asked what compliments made the strongest impression on him or her. This is an exercise to notice how much harder it sometimes is to (continuously) give compliments to people who tell something negative. Ask your supervisees also about their thoughts whether they think person 1 or person 2 needs the compliments the most.

---

4. Discuss Your Best Session

Invite supervisees to discuss their best session in pairs (each person gets 10–15 minutes). Their best experiences are discussed with a focus on what they did to make it such a good session. Pay attention to all the details of the interventions, which may take the form of exceptions that may be repeated. This discussion also enhances the liveliness and atmosphere of the supervision. Questions are:

- What was your best session recently?
- What made it such a good session?
- How exactly did you do that?
- What does that say about you?
- How would you be able to do that more often?

5. Maximize Successes

You can do this in an abbreviated form, in which all supervisees concisely describe a recent success. This application can also be used as a warming up for one of the other variants. In the long version just one or a few successes are probed (roughly 20 minutes are allotted to each case). The five steps are as follows:

1. All supervisees briefly mention a success. A few successes are chosen for further discussion, depending on how much time is available;

2. For each successful case the supervisees ask each other questions, and together they examine what the success entails exactly, what helpful interventions have been applied, and what the success signifies for the supervisee and his or her client;
3. The supervisees take turns complimenting the supervisee who presented the case on what he or she did well and on other things about the presenter that they respect and value;
4. Each supervisee briefly relates what he or she has learned from discussing the successful case and how he or she may put that knowledge to use;
5. All supervisees indicate what about the session they considered useful and beneficial and which of those things they might implement. Then the session is concluded or another case is presented.

6. Pass on Competencies to Each Other

In supervision the supervisees pair up to explore each other's competence. For this exercise it must be possible to divide the group by four persons. The steps go as follows:

1. Everyone thinks back to a (recent) session success;
2. In pairs: One member of the pair interviews his or her colleague to find out what worked. What exactly did your colleague do to help their client(s) to be successful? The colleague subsequently interviews the other person to find out what worked for him or her (2 × 7 minutes);
3. With four persons: Supervisees share their colleague's success factors with two other colleagues (10 minutes).

With this exercise the supervisees hear four success stories in quick succession: their own story, the story of the colleague they interviewed, and the stories of two other colleagues. In addition, this application allows for some physical activity, as supervisees mingle with their colleagues to recount their partner's success factors.

7. Ask the Four Basic Solution-focused Questions

When a supervisee wants to talk about a case, ask the four basic solution-focused questions:

1. What are your best hopes?
2. What difference will that make?
3. What is working?
4. What will be the next signs of progress? or What will be your next step?

When supervisees answer these basic questions, often the case no longer needs to be discussed.

Case 13 **At Least Ten Things**

A supervisor invites her supervisee to prepare, as a homework task for the next session two weeks later, a list with at least ten things that work well in her job, so she can name them in the next session. If she cannot list at least ten things, she may ask her colleagues or family members what else works well, so as to be able to come up with at least ten things. In the session after that she might even able to list twelve things.

Making lists challenges supervisees to ponder thoroughly and produce more creative ideas than they would have come up with otherwise (see Cases 14 and 15 later in this chapter).

8. Interview Each Other About Satisfaction and Capacities

Invite supervisees to interview each other in pairs about their satisfaction and capacities. By asking the follow-up question "What else," they invite each other to think again, which sometimes brings about nice surprises. The steps are as follows:

- What are you satisfied with in how you have worked since …(the last few months, start of the year, the summer)?
- What else are you satisfied with?
- What else?

Then supervisees invite each other to talk about:

- What did you notice about yourself and your capacities that you are pleased about?
- What else did you notice?
- What else?

Then they ask each other questions about their preferred future:

- How will you notice in the next three months that things are going well at work?
- How else will you notice?
- How else?

9. Ask Supervisees What They Have Done That is Good for Them

Ask supervisees which four things, at least, they have done today that are good for them:

- What have you done so far today that's good for you?
- What else have you done so far today that's good for you?

- What else?
- What else?

You may also ask them at the end of the supervision session what they have done during the session that was good for them, or else what they plan to do the rest of the day that is good for them.

10. Report a *Sparkling Moment*

Invite supervisees to report a recent sparkling moment in their work:
- Think about one of the sparkling moments in your work in the past few weeks – a moment when you felt at your best;
- How come? What was it that made the moment sparkle for you?
- What are you most satisfied with when you think back to that moment?
- What could others (colleagues or clients) have thought about you if they would have seen that moment?
- When these qualities play an even bigger role in your work, who would be the first to notice this? How would they notice? What difference will that make?
- What small step might you take to increase the prospect of (even) more sparkling moments?

11. Imagine *You At Your Best*

Invite supervisees to imagine themselves at their best. You might say to them: "Think of a specific time, recently or awhile back, when you were *at your best*. You were feeling and acting at a high level. You felt like you were expressing your authentic self, being who are. Develop a story for that experience or that moment in time. Give the story a beginning, middle, and end. You might take the approach of replaying and reliving the positive experience just as if you were watching a movie of it. Reexperiencing and savoring moments like this in your mind can lead to greater happiness and a greater chance that you will savor future moments as they happen in the present. Research has shown it is most beneficial to keep this in the mind, however, you might find it useful to jot down a few highlights."

12. Visualize *Your Best Possible Self*

Invite supervisees to visualize their *Best possible self.* You may introduce it by saying: "Take a moment to imagine a future in which you are bringing forward your best possible self. Visualize a best possible self that is very pleasing to you and that you are interested in. Imagine you have worked hard and succeeded at accomplishing your life goals. You might think of this as the realization of your life dreams and of your own best potentials. The point is not to think of unrealistic fantasies, rather, things that are positive, attainable, and within reason. After you get a fairly clear image, write about the details below. Writing your thoughts and hopes down helps to create a logical structure and helps you move from the realm of foggy ideas and fragmented thoughts to concrete, real possibilities." Research shows this is a useful exercise in helping individuals with goal-setting and building optimism and hope.

13. Design a *Certificate of Competence*

Invite supervisees to pair up and help each other to make a *certificate of competence* (or interview your individual supervisee) using the next seven questions (based on the work of John Wheeler, see www.johnwheeler.co.uk):

1. When I do my work I take my inspiration from the following people:

   ....

2. These people have taught me that when I do my work it is most important to remember the following:

   ....

3. These are the people who encourage me to do the work I do:

   ....

4. They encouraged me to do this work because they noticed the following about me:

   ....

5. When I do my work, the people I deal with are likely to appreciate that I have the following qualities and abilities:

   ....

6. These are the people in my support network who know I have these qualities and abilities:

   ....

7. If I am under pressure at work and can only remember one quality or ability it should be this:

   ....

14. Ask About Success, Talent, and Ambition

At the start of supervision invite supervisees to talk about their successes, talents, and ambitions. When there is a group or peer supervision a nice way to start is to invite all participants to interview each other in pairs for 3–5 minutes each and then to invite them to introduce the other person briefly (1 minute) to the group based on their success, talent, and ambition.

15. Use *Positive Gossip*

Invite supervisees to gossip positively in triplets about each other. Instead of the usual negative gossip positive gossip is focusing on discussing positive aspects and successes of the colleague. Supervisees 1 and 2 use positive gossip together about Supervisee 3, as if he or she is not there and cannot hear it. This Supervisee 3 is not allowed to react and sits with his or her back towards the two colleagues in order to avoid eye contact. Every 2 minutes they change roles, so that in three rounds all supervisees have a turn. Although some supervisees sometimes feel a little awkward at first, they appreciate hearing so many positive things about themselves (which they usually do not hear).

16. A Variation of Positive Gossip

Invite supervisees to sit in groups of five to six people and think about one of their favorite clients. They are then invited to pretend to be that favorite client and to sit in a waiting room with other clients. They then use positive gossip about their supervisor/social worker/coach/ mediator/chef (which means they gossip about themselves). Some people are initially ill at ease but after a while they loosen up and there is a lot of laughter.

17. Make Lists

Remember the song *Fifty ways to leave your lover* by Paul Simon? Inviting supervisees to make lists is always fun and at the same time challenging. Below are five assignments, each one sums up ten positive things, so 5 × 10 = 50 positive things, to find happiness. It is fun to discuss these with the supervisor or fellow supervisees. It is also nice to hear which positive things the others mention. This may bring new ideas forward about their own positive sides.
1.   List ten positive traits of yourself.
2.   List ten successes in your life and/or work.
3.   List ten ways in which you are nice towards others.
4.   List ten strokes of luck in your life and/or work.
5.   List ten ways you are supported by others.

Case 14 **Making Lists**

The supervisee lets out a deep sigh and says: "I am not sure I can go on much longer ... my job is hard-going, I have small children at home, and a training course, and this supervision, phew." The supervisor acknowledges the gravity of the situation by saying she can imagine that it must feel like a heavy burden. Then she asks her supervisee to describe 50 ways how she copes with this situation.

The supervisee hears: "Five ways?"

"No, 50 ways," replies the supervisor. "Would you like to start in this session or would you prefer to do this as a homework task?"

The supervisee looks at the supervisor incredulously, but then begins to search for the ways in which she copes. How does she manage? She sometimes goes to bed at the same time as her children to catch up some sleep. She still manages to go to the gym twice a week, even though she doesn't want to and would prefer to sit on the couch watching TV. During the process of finding the fifty things that work or may work, her attitude changes: she straightens her back and occasionally a smile pops up on her face. At the end of the session she has written down 43 ways and says no doubt she will find the other seven at home.

The supervisor compliments her on the great list. When she gives feedback to the supervisor she says: "This session showed me that it's not a question of *whether* I can go on and cope, because now I know I can, but *how* I do that."

Case 15 **More Lists**

A supervisee applied for a job as a psychologist. She received an invitation for an interview; quite an achievement in view of the large number of applicants. "How do I present myself next week?" she wonders. The supervisor proposes that she sits down the evening prior to the interview with a good friend and produce a list with a 100 reasons why they should choose her for the job. The friend, with whom she made the appointment, canceled it because he was ill, so she produces the list herself the evening before the meeting. She came up with 64 reasons and got the job. We will never know for sure if making the list contributed to her success, but she told the supervisor afterwards that she went through the interview with more self-confidence.

18. Make an Accordion With Compliments

Ask supervisees to write their name at the top of a piece of paper and to pass this paper on to the person beside them. Everyone writes on the piece of paper what strengths he or she sees in the person whose name is on top of the paper and then gives the paper to their neighbor. At the end the paper arrives back at the person whose name is on top of the paper, full of compliments. One might fold the paper like an accordion after each compliment, so that no one can see each other's comments.

19. Create an *Appreciation Wall*

Invite supervisees to create an *appreciation wall*. It's a fun way to give feed-back to each other. It captures each other's strengths and promotes relation-ships. Create the appreciation wall as follows:

- Write in large letters at the top of a large sheet of paper: "What we value about each other."
- Divide the paper into squares for all those present.
- Invite everyone to grab a pen and to write in each box (or use post-its) what they appreciate about their colleagues.
- Observe together what everyone has written down and ask them to share some explanations and small examples.

Summary

- Finding competence is an important pillar in positive supervision. "What works (already)?" is the question that is helpful in this quest. In this way the road already traveled is considered (and not just the road ahead), which creates positive emotions and an increase in intrinsic motivation. Taking the VIA Survey of Character Strengths to discover the top five signature character strengths is another way to find com-petencies.
- By finding exceptions to the problem competencies are also detected. Useful questions are: "When is the problem not there or less, or, when is there already a little piece of the preferred future you described?" followed by: "How do(did) you do that?"
- In addition nineteen other ways to find the supervisees' competencies are described.

Chapter 5
Pillar 3: Working on Progress

Seeing yourself as you want to be is the key to personal growth.
Unknown

This chapter focuses on Pillar 3: working on (further) progress by building on previous successes. The fourth and last of the solution-oriented basic questions is: "What will be next signs of progress?" Or more directly: "What will be your (small) next step?" In this instance the supervisees don't have to start from zero (see Chapter 4). In an earlier chapter it was outlined that building on successes is different from solving problems.

Sometimes supervisors are concerned about shortcomings in the knowledge or competence of their supervisees. It is important that the supervisors have a *growth mindset*: the assumption that their own competence and that of their supervisees is not stable, and can be enhanced. More about the *growth mindset* can be found later in this chapter. You will also find a description of the usefulness of scaling questions. Scaling questions can simplify complicated and complex things. Scaling questions can be about progress towards the preferred future (the goal), about confidence, hope, and motivation. In addition you find twenty further ideas on how to build on successes and dissolve an impasse.

It is not only humans who think that building success is important, but also some animals who consider it to be *the most important subject of all*. In *Winnie-the-Pooh on Success*, the wise Stranger tells the animals how they can become successful:

"What does the success formula taste like?"

"It's not that kind of formula, Silly Bear," said The Stranger. He took a sheet of paper out of his case and began writing on it. When he finished, he turned it around and showed it to his friends. This is what he had written:

Select a Dream

Use your dreams to set a Goal

Create a Plan

Consider Resources

Enhance Skills and Abilities

Spend time Wisely

Start! Get Organized and Go

"It spells Suchness!" shouted Piglet.

"Close, Piglet," said The Stranger. "It spells Success."

(Allen & Allen, 1997, p. 17)

Building on Successes

Building on successes means building on what already works. Walter and Peller (2000) describe how they are looking for *signals* or *signs of progress* in psychotherapy: "What will be some of the signals that you are more relaxed?"; "What will be the first sign that you are improving?"; "What will be more signs that things (between the two of you) are better?"; "And what will be another sign of that?" These signals don't show yet who is in charge of the improvement. Therefore, it may be good to add: "What will be *your* next (small) step?" This makes clear that it is up to the client to make a change. The words *small step* signifies that *baby steps*" are needed, steps that are small enough to ensure that the supervisees are successful, instead of failing due to a step that turns out to be too big. Questions like: "What would be the smallest step you can take?"; "What will be the easiest step for you?" are often helpful.

First ask supervisees where on the scale 10–0 they want to end and if there is a desire or need for progress. Sometimes supervisees just want to maintain the results and there is no need – for now – for further progress. In that case the scaling question about progress changes into questions about how to maintain the achieved results (see Chapter 7).

Growth Mindset

Sometimes supervisors are concerned about the shortcomings of their supervisees. Selekman and Todd (1995) argue that learning is most effective and new information is processed best when supervisees are asking for it themselves. Supervisors should not think too quickly that supervisees don't know the right answers or are short in certain abilities.

In addition, supervisors should believe in the possibility of developing competencies in themselves and their supervisees through effort and experience. Research shows that belief in the development of capacities is an important precondition for the actual development of those capacities. We call this a *growth mindset*. Dweck (2006) conducted research into what people believe about the development of capacities. She differentiates two types of beliefs: a *fixed mindset* and a *growth mindset*. People with a fixed mindset believe that capacities, such as intelligence, are innate, fixed, and unchangeable. People with a *growth mindset* see abilities as developable.

What people believe largely determines their actions. People with a fixed mindset often focus strongly on performance by showing their competence and less on the process of improving. As a result, they often don't get any further than where they are. People with a growth mindset focus primarily on the process to improve at a certain competence, in this way they make progress. Someone with a fixed mindset could avoid problems, because problems could prove that he or she is not capable, if the problem is not solved. Someone with a growth mindset wants to solve problems, because in that way he or she can improve their skills. Success by others can be seen as a threat to a person with a fixed mindset, whereas a person with a growth mindset would experience this as inspiring. This ties in with my idea that people like to work on *becoming better* at certain competencies (see Chapter 4).

From the viewpoint of positive supervision, it is usually not necessary to be taught new things. One *becomes better* at recognizing what is already there (exceptions) or one *remembers better* in terms of doing something, if they have forgotten it temporarily. Also, there doesn't have to be something wrong with you before you can become better at something. In other words, *you don't have to be ill to get better.* The story about the car wash, described in the previous chapter, shows how the motivation to achieve a certain goal increases when you have already traveled a part of the journey. Here the conclusion of the experiment is repeated: *"When soliciting another person for help with anything, you should try to point out how that person has already taken steps towards the completion of that task."*

Usefulness of Scaling Questions

The supervisors can help supervisees to express complex, intuitive observations about their experiences and estimates of future possibilities by means of scaling questions. Scaling questions invite supervisees to put their observations, impressions, and predictions on a scale from 10–0. For example, you may ask your supervisees: "On a scale from 10–0, where 10 means you are confident that you can reach your goal and 0 means you are not confident at all, where would you say you are now?" Scaling questions can be used after the goal is formulated or exceptions are found, to keep track of the progress the supervisees are making. Scaling questions can function as the starting point for *successive approximation*, also known as *shaping*. This is a form of operant conditioning, in which the increasingly accurate approximations of a desired response are reinforced.

The supervisors might first ask if the supervisees know how to work with scales and scaling questions. Frequently used scaling questions are:

- When the goal you want to reach is at 10 and the opposite is 0, where are you now on this scale?
- Where would your clients say you are now on the scale?
- How do you manage to be at that point?
- What would your clients say about how you manage to be there?
- How is it that the point is not lower that it is?
- Where would you like to be on the scale at the end of this supervision?
- How will a point higher on the scale look to you?
- What will be different when you are a point higher? What will you be doing differently?
- What will others (clients, colleagues) see you doing differently at one point higher on the scale?
- How can you reach a point higher?
- What would your clients say about how you could reach one point higher?
- Who or what can help you to get there?

These scaling questions are about progress towards the preferred future. They can be posed again in each subsequent session or after some sessions: "Where are you now on the scale of 10–0?"; "How did you get there?" Scaling questions can also be about motivation, hope, and confidence. "How motivated are you to come to this supervision, as 10 means you're willing to do anything for it and 0 means the opposite?" or "How much confidence do you have that you will achieve your goal, where 10 means you are very confident and 0 means the opposite?"

When supervisees give a high score on the scale, they are asked: "How do you manage to be at such a high point on the scale?" and: "What is in that number?" If supervisees are lower on the scale they are asked: "How come it is not less?"; "Suppose you would be a little higher on the scale, what will you do differently then?" and: "What would your clients say you would be doing differently then?"

Again, the perspective of their clients is most important and not the perspective of the supervisees themselves (see Chapter 1 and 4). From this perspective the following scaling questions may be asked:

- What will *your client say* with regard to where the best session was on a scale of 10–0?
- What will *your client say* about what's in that point (and it's not lower)?
- What will *your client say* about how you have been helpful on a scale of 10–0?
- What will *your client say* about the progress that has been made?
- What will *your client say* about what one point higher will look like?
- What will *your client say* about how he or she can attain one point higher?
- If the rating is low: what will *your client say* that you should do differently in order to be more helpful?
- If the rating is high: where does *the client think* he or she is on a scale of 10–0? What will he or she say about how they managed to do that and how you have been helpful?
- What will *your client say* about when he or she can finish the sessions with you?

Dissolving Stagnation

Of course positive supervision is not just about strengths and what works. Many supervisees also want to talk about their own problems and the impasses or stagnation in their treatments, particularly when they think or the supervisor thinks this is the only purpose of supervision. Earlier it was outlined that most models of supervision are still problem-focused, with the objective of solving problems and repairing what is wrong. Positive supervision goes beyond problem solving and repairing and builds on solutions and what works. Bannink (2010b, 2013, 2014b) describes seven ways to bring about an impasse or failure, including: goal formulation in negative terms, anticipation of failure, continuing with an approach that doesn't work, not taking into account the motivation of the client, and so on.

Sometimes there is also an impasse in supervision. Walter and Peller (1992) offer some questions to use in situations where there seem to be no progress:

- Who wants to change?;
- What is the supervisees' goal? The supervisees should want to reach their goal more than the supervisors and speak more than the supervisors;
- Do you have a goal and not a wish? Is the goal well defined and within the control of the supervisees?;
- Are you and the supervisees looking for too much too fast? Try looking for a smaller change;
- Are the supervisees not doing the tasks which you expected them to do? In this case, provide some feedback for them to think about or observe rather than an action-oriented task;
- If you have gone through all the above steps and the impasse remains, is there something you should do differently? Sometimes we are too close to the trees to see the forest and may not recognize a nonproductive pattern between the supervisees and us as supervisors. A team or consultant may be helpful to provide a more detached frame of reference.

Exercise 24 Could It Be Worse?

Pose this question to your (pessimistic) supervisees: "Could the situation be worse?" If they give an affirmative answer to this – which is almost always the case – ask them how it is not worse than it is, and how they made that happen. In the answer unexpected competencies may come to light, which make it easier to bring about progress at a later stage.

Could it be worse? In the 1960s, an executive at IBM made a decision that ended up losing the company 10 million US dollars. The CEO of IBM summoned the offending executive to his office at corporate headquarters. A journalist described what happened next: As the executive cowered, the CEO asked, "Do you know why I've asked you here?" The man replied: "I assume I'm here so you can fire me." The CEO looked surprised. "Fire you?" he asked. "Of course not. I just spent 10 million dollars educating you."

Berg and Steiner (2003) suggest the following questions for therapists if there has been no progress in working with their clients. I think these questions also apply to supervisors, taking the perspective or their supervisees:

- If I were to ask my supervisees how my contribution has helped, even if only a little bit, what would they respond?

- What do my supervisees consider to be a sign of a successful outcome?
- How realistic is that outcome?
- What do I as their supervisor consider to be a sign of success?
- If my supervisees' and my views differ, what needs to be done so that we can work on the same goal?
- On a scale of 0–10, where 10 means great progress and 0 means no progress at all, where would my supervisees say they are right now? What needs to happen to bring my supervisees one point closer to 10?

(Berg & Steiner, 2003, p. 223)

The progress made by supervisees may again be assessed by means of scaling questions, which may be asked of both the supervisees and also of important people in their environment. Sometimes the goal may change over time and more possibilities show up than were first anticipated.

In case of an impasse sometimes the ideas and convictions of the supervisors or their supervisees are impeding the progress. Which attitudes are perpetuating the impasse? The central point is that the motivation that the supervisors attribute to the supervisees (or the supervisees attribute to the clients) carries over into the alliance. It is important to examine whether a different interpretation of the behavior and the motives of the supervisees (or clients) might break the impasse. *Positive relabeling* and *reinterpretation* can be useful. What may constitute another credible explanation for the supervisees' or their clients' behavior? Based on this what would the supervisors or supervisees do differently during the session and how might it then run more smoothly? This model appeals to the supervisors' or supervisees' self-reflectiveness.

- What exactly do you and your supervisees (or clients) do during the session?
- What motivation would you say that the supervisees (or clients) have, if you were to vent your frustrations to a colleague?
- How does your interpretation cause you to react in the same manner?
- How might you look at it differently? What more positive motivation might the supervisees (or clients) have?
- What if you were to act in accordance with a different interpretation, what would you do differently?
- What difference will that make? How will the next session go better?

Twenty Ways to Work on Progress

Below you find twenty different applications to work on (further) progress.

1. Discuss Your Most Challenging Case

With this application the most difficult – better still: most challenging – case is presented and a limited amount of time is allotted to each case (5 minutes maximum). This exercise can be done in pairs or in groups, with everyone taking a turn.

The goal is to go through a large number of cases in a short amount of time. This method takes up little time and calls for a lot of input. The focus is on how the supervisees can move up one point on the scale (see Chapter 8). Background information about the case is unnecessary; what matters is what the supervisees presenting the case are able or willing to do to move one point higher on the scale. With challenging cases there is almost always an impasse or a negative alliance with the clients. The objective is for the supervisees to recognize small improvements. Ask each other the following question: "Suppose the next session ends one point higher on the scale than the last one, what will you have done differently?" Note that this question is not about what the clients should do differently.

A more elaborate version is as follows:
- How would you rate the last session, if 10 means that the session went really well and 0 means the opposite?
- How come you give this rating and not a lower one?
- When the next session ends one point higher on the scale, what will you have done differently to achieve this?
- What ideas does everyone else have?

These questions may be repeated for everyone's second most challenging case. This ensures that many cases can be discussed in a short period of time.

2. Practice Scaling Questions

Invite supervisees to interview each other (or interview your individual supervisee) about something that is useful for them and can be put on a scale (I want progress in ……). The content may remain secret.
- Find at least 10 things that (already) work.
- What point on the scale would the supervisee say s/he is at now, where 10 means their goal is completely reached and 0 means the opposite.
- Find four or five signs of (further) progress.

For example, ask: "When you are a point higher on the scale, what would you notice that is different?"; "What else will be different?"; "What will you be doing differently?" Change roles after 20 minutes when working in pairs.

3. Scale Walk

Many people, especially young ones, prefer to walk together outside, moving around a bit and not having to look at each other all the time. While walking along an imaginary line, one can ask scaling questions. The supervisees define the topic for their scale walk (e.g., progress in …).

1. Supervisees find a place for their scale walk (inside or outside).
   Supervisor: "Where is 10 on the scale, where is 0 on the scale?"
2. Supervisor asks the supervisees how high up they want to get on the scale and invites them to explore this goal on the scale by stepping on the spot which represents that goal for them.
   Supervisor: "Now that you have reached your goal, what capabilities and resources do you notice about yourself?"; "What do you do differently now?"; "What else?"; "How do others notice?"
3. Supervisor then invites the supervisees to look at things from a more distant perspective by stepping outside the scale.
   Supervisor: "Where would you say you are right now on your scale?"
4. Supervisees are asked to step on to their position on the scale which represents where they are now.
   Supervisor: "Looking back at the distance you have already traveled from 0 till now, what are some of the milestones and major lessons learned?"; "What are you particularly proud of about these developments?"; "How did you manage to do that?"; "What point would you say you are at right now on the scale?"
5. Supervisor now invites the supervisees to take a next step into their own future by moving along the scale.
   Supervisor: "Where on the scale will you stand so you notice the difference?" (Supervisees step on to that next point).
   Supervisor: "What differences do you start to notice now that you are on this point?"; "What resources do you have at this point?"; "What resources do you have now, that you did not have before?"; "How do you think and act differently now that you are here?"; "What else do you notice about being at this point?"
6. Step by step the supervisor invites the supervisees to explore further points on the scale.
   Supervisor: "What other spot on the scale might be interesting for you to explore next?" (Supervisees step onto that next point). "What differences do you notice at this point?"; "What else do you or others notice that is different?"; "What is your most surprising discovery about this point?"
7. Supervisees and supervisor move up the scale as far as the supervisees want to explore.

Scale walking can also be done with more than one person at a time, for example, with a team or in peer supervision when there is a common goal.

4. Create a Five-year Plan

Invite supervisees to look further ahead than they are probably used to by making a *five-year plan*. Have them divide a big sheet of paper into squares. On the vertical axis subgoals are written, about work, family, money, relationships, etc., one per square. On the horizontal axis they write the timeline in each box (six months, one year, two years, etc.,– whatever measure works for them). First the supervisees write where they want to be in five years time for all the sub goals. They start at the furthest point in time, not the closest. Once those boxes are filled then they work backwards and think about where they should be after three years, in order to reach the goal at the end of the five years. Where should they be after one year? And two years? The five-year plan helps the supervisee to set realistic goals in a time frame, so it becomes clear which steps should be taken to stay on track and to reach the goals in five years.

5. Create Challenges

Invite supervisees for 10 minutes (in pairs or in two groups) to come up with some challenging expressions used by their clients. Divide the supervisees in two groups and ask each group to make a list of (five or ten) difficult phrases and give the list to the other group. Invite each group in turn to formulate the best possible responses to the expressions they received and share these. Once the first group is finished the second group contributes their responses or they may take turns.

6. Follow the Steps of Reteaming

Furman and Aloha (2007) describe a solution-focused method called *reteaming*, which consists of 12 consecutive, logical steps intended to help individuals (including supervisees) as well as groups to change for the better by facilitating the setting of goals, and increasing and enhancing both the motivation and the cooperation needed to achieve them. Reteaming generates hope and optimism, builds motivation, and enhances creativity and cooperation between people. In reteaming change is seen as a collective process, something done together with others. Individuals, in most cases, need help, support, and encouragement from others in order to change. The twelve steps are: (1) describe your dream, (2) identify a goal, (3) recruit supporters, (4) highlight the benefit of the goal, (5) recognize progress already made, (6) picture forthcoming progress, (7) acknowledge the challenge, (8) find grounds for confidence, (9) make promises to others that you will succeed, (10) follow up your progress, (11) prepare for possible setbacks, and (12) celebrate success and acknowledge your supporters.

7. Pretend the Goal Is Achieved

Invite supervisees, when they have a clear view of their preferred future, *to pretend* their goal has been achieved. To practice what this feels like they may, for example, choose one morning in their workweek or a session with a client to behave as if their goal has been achieved. If the *miracle question* has been asked during supervision (see Chapter 3) then the supervisee may act *as if* (part of) the miracle has happened. An alternative is to invite supervisees to pretend to be one point higher on the scale than is the case in reality and observe the differences in their mood and behavior. These behavioral experiments are often useful and fun to do; the objective is always to look for the positive differences.

8. Make a Prediction

Invite supervisees to *make a prediction* about how they will function at work the next day. Ask them to assign a number from 10–0 to the predicted state of being. At the end of the following day ask them to observe whether their prediction was correct. If yes: how did they predict their functioning so well? If the number they gave was lower than the next day turned out: what went better than predicted and how did they do that? If the number they gave was higher than the next day turned out: what did they do so the number did not turn out to be lower than it was? How can they get a higher number? Then invite them to make another prediction for the day after that and so on. Doing this exercise often leads to surprising results.

9. Pay Attention to What You Are Doing When You Overcome the Urge to ...

Give this task to supervisees to help them to find and use exceptions to a problem. It works well with negative habits, such as procrastination, alcohol or drug abuse, smoking, obsessive-compulsive behavior, perfectionism etc.

There are always situations when the problem is not there, or exists to a lesser extent. Ask the supervisees to think of such occasions. Once these exceptions are noticed they can become part of the repertoire of the supervisees and can be used again in other situations. The focus is on what supervisees do that is working instead of what isn't working and needs to be changed. You may also ask supervisees to share what they know about how other people overcome the urge to perpetuate a negative habit, or ask other supervisees present to talk about what works for them.

Case 16   Observe Exceptions

A supervisee wants to become less of a perfectionist. She sets very high standards for herself, especially concerning her work. At home she is less of a perfectionist. This proves that there are exceptions to the problem, outside of her work. Her supervisor could have asked more questions about those exceptions, but opts for a slightly different approach in finding exceptions. The supervisor asks the supervisee: "When are there times at work when you are slightly less perfectionistic and yet still successful in what you do?" The supervisee considers this a difficult question and no easy answer pops up.

Because the supervisee is interested in monitoring this kind of exception, she accepts a homework suggestion to observe when these moments of reduced perfectionism (instead she wants to be relaxed and mindful) arise. She discovers that of course these exceptions also occur at work and she figures out how she manages to do her best with less fastidiousness. Sometimes she manages to leave unfinished work and go home because she gives priority to sports. Sometimes she is successful in relaxing her standards because she says to herself that it doesn't always have to be perfect and that a little bit less perfection is good enough. With this awareness the solutions are already present: she will do more of what works and continue to observe what else works.

10. Externalize the Problem

If supervisees want to discuss their own problem, externalizing the problem might be a good choice. This practice helps the supervisees to see their problem as something that is separate from them, something that influences them, but that doesn't control their lives at all times. First the problem is given a name (X). The question for the supervisees is: "What do you call the thing that troubles you?" X may be: perfectionism, depression, irritation, etc. Then the supervisor asks the following (scaling) questions:

- Where do you rate yourself today on the scale of control (10 means you have total control, 0 means the opposite)?
- If the rating is higher than the previous rating: "How did you manage to reach a higher point on the scale?" and: "What differences do you notice?"
- If the rating is the same as the previous rating: "How did you manage to maintain the same rating?"
- If the rating is lower than the previous rating: "What did you do before to get ahead again?" or "What did you do in a comparable situation in the past that was successful?""What have important others in your life noticed about you recently?"; "How did that influence their behavior toward you?"

Also questions may be asked that position the problem as an enemy who needs to be defeated or, on the other hand, questions can be asked which uncover how the supervisees may become friends with this problem (Bannink, 2010b. 2013).

11. Do More of What Works

Invite supervisees to give a detailed description of everything that works for them (even just a little bit) when dealing with a problem. This list can include everything that has worked in the past or is working now. In these descriptions the keys to solutions and change are already present. Often supervisees don't have to do anything different to make progress possible and the supervisor or colleagues in peer supervision don't have to give advice or suggestions (just encouragement).

12. Do Something Different

Einstein stated that insanity is doing the same thing over and over again (see Chapter 6). If something is not working, stop doing it and do something else. If there is no progress, discuss this with your supervisees. Invite them to come up with creative ideas about what they could do differently and find out what difference this makes. The same principle applies as in the previous application: the supervisor or colleagues don't have to give advice or suggestions. If something works better, they should do more of it, if not, they should think of something else.

13. Observe What Doesn't Have to Change

Often supervisors and supervisees only focus on things they want to change or need to be changed. This may cause dissatisfaction or uncertainty about the supervisees' existing competencies. Invite them to observe what doesn't have to change, because it is OK as it is. Or invite them to observe what they will not even allow to change, because they are pleased about it.

14. Use Strengths

Invite supervisees to take the Values in Action (VIA) Survey of Character Strengths (see Chapter 4, at www.authentichappiness.org). Then discuss their top 5 of signature strengths. Invite them to observe how they can apply these strengths in their work (even) more than they already do, or how they can apply these strengths in a new area in their work or life. This will generate more flow (Bannink, 2009a) and supervisees will feel more competent.

15. Use *OASIS*

The OASIS model, as described in Table 4, can be used in group or peer supervision.

Table 4. OASIS model

	Group	Supervisee presenting case (A)
Opening	One round of questions	Answers questions
Appreciation	One round of appreciation about what A does, clients do	Listens
Suggestions	One round: "If I was you, I'd..."	Listens
Impact	Listens	Talks about the impact of the process
Step	Listens	Defines one first step

16. Challenge negative thoughts

This activity is about contradicting negative thoughts as quickly as possible. Challenging their negative reflections may be useful for supervisees. Ask supervisees to write down the typical negative thoughts that pop up in their mind sometimes, such as: "This will never work" or "I will never be a good therapist." The idea is to write these thoughts on index cards. After they have written the cards with some of their regular negative thoughts, they pick one up at random and read it out loud. Then the others in the group rapidly dispute the negative beliefs with every possible argument each person can come up with. This is called: *Rapid Fire Facts*: the supervisees rapidly fire contradicting positive facts at the negative sentence. When they run out of facts, the supervisee picks another card and the others repeat the positive rapid-fire facts. Coming up with contradictory facts will get easier and easier with each card. With this tool the supervisees learn to become adept at contradicting their negative thoughts. This exercise can also be done with an individual supervisee.

17. Go to Chapter 2

Invite supervisees to imagine that their life is a book made up of many chapters. Say: "If you were to write the story of your life as an exercise then, in this exercise, you should begin with the second chapter instead of beginning at Chapter 1.

In starting with Chapter 2, any problems which you are currently experiencing, can be omitted. What positive differences would there be in the description of your life? Which people would you omit and which people would you include as part of Chapter 2? Which strengths and resources do you have in Chapter 2? Which good ideas from Chapter 2 could you be using already?"

18. Visit a Store

In the Netherlands there is a little rhyme about a store where you can buy anything you want (*Winkel van Sinkel*). You may buy a pound of courage, a lion that protects you against danger or a balance to weigh every request first before you say yes or no. Invite supervisees to enter this store, have a good look around and choose one or more things that may help them to reach their goal or solve their problem. Everything is free and you can always return and change any item, if it doesn't suit you. What is special about this store is that you may also leave behind anything that you don't need anymore, but someone else may find useful, such as a bag filled with perfectionism. Invite supervisees to use their new items and observe how these items may help them move forward.

> ### Case 17 Visit a Store
>
> A supervisee told her supervisor that she feels very anxious when doing exams. Because this fear is withholding her career, she would like to get some help from her supervisor. The supervisor proposes that the woman visit the Winkel van Sinkel (general store). After she has looked around a bit, the supervisee chooses three items: a beautiful white embroidered pillow on which she can lay down her head when she is tired; a black panther who will enter the scary exam forest first; and a little angel on her right shoulder that compliments her (instead of a little devil on her left shoulder that always criticizes her). She chooses not to leave anything behind in the store. At home the supervisee practices with the pillow, panther, and angel by rehearsing how she will be able to finish her exams. Later on she brings her three imaginary items with her to her next exams and succeeds in passing them.

19. Make it Easy for Yourself

Invite supervisees to make it difficult for themselves by doing things they don't want to do and easy for themselves by doing things they want to do. To gain more control over things they don't want, they may, for example, only smoke in an unattractive environment, or ensure that they don't buy certain foods, cigarettes, or drugs if they know it will be difficult not to use them. To encourage them to do things they do want, invite them to go to the gym around the corner, instead of having to drive a long way to get there. It is a misunderstanding that people need a lot of willpower to do less of what they don't want to do. A good plan and support from others are far more important (see finding supporters in *reteaming*, earlier in this Chapter).

20. Create a Mind Map

Supervisees may make a *mind map* about a presented problem and/or about the solutions for that problem. Everyone is invited to write on a large sheet of paper with colored pencils and felt-tip pens and draw what comes to their minds following the writing of a word by a member of the group. Often this results in a surprising number of creative ideas, which can help overcome impasses and through which progress can be achieved.

Summary

- Positive supervision builds on previous successes and goes beyond just solving problems.
- Supervisors should have a *growth mindset*, relying on increasing the capacities of themselves and their supervisees.
- The usefulness of scaling questions is highlighted.
- To avoid and/or dissolve impasse supervisors and their supervisees may answer specific questions, making progress possible again.
- Twenty other ways to work on (further) progress are discussed.

Chapter 6
Pillar 4: Reflection

> *Insanity is doing the same thing over and over again,*
> *expecting different results*
> Albert Einstein

This chapter focuses on Pillar 4: Reflection. Reflection may take place at the end of every session or after a few sessions, by both supervisors and supervisees. There are a large number of questions available for reflection on professional as well as personal performance.

It is well known that not all supervisors and supervisees are equally good and, of course, the same applies to supervisees. Who are the *super-supervisors*, and who are the *super-supervisees*? What do they do differently and in what way are they especially better than their average colleagues? In this chapter you will find the answer, which you may use to your advantage. You also find 22 applications for reflection. It is not only advisable for supervisors or supervisees to reflect on their sessions but also to invite their supervisees (or their clients) to give feedback.

The Importance of Reflection

In supervision, stimulation and guidance of experiential learning is important. Reflection is an essential skill, which invites supervisors and supervisees to support their decision-making. Besides reflection on stagnation or failure, reflection on successes is advisable. Both supervisors and supervisees do well to reflect on every session – short if time is tight, more extensive if possible. Useful questions are:
- What worked and will I do again in a similar situation?
- What didn't work and will I do differently in a similar situation?

After every session in positive supervision one may pose some questions, which help to reflect on his or her own part of the session. This ensures that competencies can be further developed and one can learn from (or rather: become better at) the things that didn't go well.

Here are a number of questions for supervisors (about their supervisees) and supervisees (about their clients) to reflect on their *professional performance*:

- Suppose I was to conduct this session again, what would I do again?
- Suppose I were to conduct this session again, what would I do differently or better next time?
- What would the supervisee/client say I could do differently or better?
- What difference would that make for the supervisee/client?
- What difference would that make for me?
- Suppose I conduct sessions in the future with a supervisee/client who has a comparable problem. Which interventions would I use again and which wouldn't I?
- What will the supervisee/client say about how useful this session has been?
- How satisfied do I think the supervisee/client is with my performance (on a scale of 10–0)?
- What would he or she say about how I've managed to get to that point on the scale?
- What would it look like for him or her if I were one point higher on the scale?
- What difference will that make for the supervision/treatment?
- What would the supervisee/client say if I asked him or her how I could move up one point on the scale?
- How satisfied am I with my own performance (on a scale of 10–0)?
- How did I manage to get to that number?
- What do I think one point higher on the scale would look like?
- What difference will that make for the supervision/treatment?
- What or who can help me to move up one point?
- What positive aspects of this supervision/treatment stand out?
- What useful information have I received from the supervisee/client?
- On which of his or her competencies and features can I compliment the supervisee/client?
- What does the supervisee/client want to achieve in meeting with me?
- What will be the best outcome of these sessions for my supervisee/client?
- What competencies can this supervisee/client utilize to solve the problem, which brings him or her here?
- What kind of resources does the supervisee/client need from his or her environment? Which resources are already available?
- What information about or impression of this supervisee/client do I have that may help in determining his or her goal?

- What do I see in this supervisee/client (or partners, family, team) that tells me that he or she or they can reach his or her or their goal?
- If I were to make a video of how I work now and one of how I will work at the end of this supervision/treatment, which differences do I see? How will I know which video is about the end of the supervision/treatment?
- How will my colleagues know that I have reached my goal?
- How will they react? What difference will that make for them?
- How will I know I am on the right track?
- How will others know I am on the right track?
- What will be some signals that I am on the right track?
- How will I know I did this well?
- What aspects of my professional performance do I definitely want to maintain?

Some questions for reflection on their *personal performance* are:
- When I experience problems on a personal level, what works best in helping me overcoming them?
- What resources do I have at my disposal in my personal life?
- What competencies and qualities do I have?
- How can I utilize them to find solutions to potential problems?
- Where would I like to be in one year, five years, or ten years?
- What would the miracle (see Chapter 3) look like for me?
- What would indicate to me that I am on the right track?
- What would indicate to important people in my life that I am on the right track?
- What would be the first small (next) step I could take on that path?
- What difference will that make to me? And to others?
- How will things change between me and important people in my life?
- What aspects of my personal life do I definitely want to maintain?

Exercise 25 Questions for Reflection

Ask yourself some of above questions after your next sessions and invite your supervisees to do the same, regardless of whether the sessions were successful or not. Explore how these questions will help you/them to become better at your/their work. Also invite your supervisees to deliver feedback more frequently: "What was important for you as a supervisee in this session?"; "What was helpful?"; "What would you rather see different?"; "What can I as your supervisor do better or differently next time?" Feedback can also be given using the Session Rating Scale (see Chapter 6).

A phenomenon in supervision is the "Dunning-Kruger effect'" named after the psychologists who studied this phenomenon. People who are competent sometimes tend to underestimate their own capacities. People who are incompetent, however, sometimes miss the metacognitive ability to see that they are not competent, as a result of which they tend to overestimate their own capacities. So when supervisees become more competent, they can feel more insecure at the same time. The reason for this is that their metacognitive ability to judge themselves increases and they will be more critical of themselves. Knowing this phenomenon exists may be helpful, because when this happens, supervisors can normalize the feelings of their supervisees: it is a normal aspect of becoming more competent.

Super-Supervisors and Super-Supervisees

It is obvious that not every professional is equally successful. As some lawyers have better results, some artists create more remarkable works of art and students perform better with some teachers than others, some supervisors also achieve better results than others. Who are those super-professionals who achieve 50% more successes and 50% or fewer dropouts?

Miller, Duncan, and Hubble (1997) found solid empirical evidence for what distinguishes highly effective therapists (which they called *supershrinks*) from other psychotherapists. This research reaches the following findings and recommendations, which are probably also applicable to supervision.

1. Don't expect too much from training and experience. Surprisingly, training, certification, supervision, years of experience, and even use of evidence-based practices do not contribute to superior performance. Research conducted over the last 30 years documents that the effectiveness rates of most clinicians plateaus very early in training, despite the fact that most professionals believe they improve with time and experience. A direct relation between supervision and a greater effectiveness in treatment has never been found (Veeninga, 2008; Veeninga & Hafkenscheid, 2010), although there is evidence that supervisees think highly of supervision. Watkins (1998) also poses that supervision is regarded as important, but that the empirical base for supervision should be enhanced; he provided some recommendations. However, there are a number of methodological problems which have to be tackled before it can be scientifically measured whether supervision is effective and if so, how this works.

2. Have faith in your own model. The faith therapists have in the treatment and the capacity of that treatment to help clients change (the *alle-*

giance), is an important quality of a competent therapist. Allegiance towards a treatment is based on the idea that if therapists are favorably disposed towards a treatment and experience the positive effects of that treatment, they will execute this treatment with more perseverance, enthusiasm, hope, and competence (Wampold, 2001).

3. Ensure a positive working relationship (the *alliance*). Research on the impact of variables in therapists' characteristics shows that competent, creative, committed therapists can smooth out any restriction on their age, gender, or colur of skin (Beutler et al., 2004). There is a consistent relationship between a positive and friendly attitude of the therapist and a positive outcome. A critical and hostile attitude has the opposite effect. Norcross (2002) found that the personality of the therapist and the alliance with their clients are far more powerful determinants of the outcome of the sessions than the choice of methodology. The therapist's degree of comfort with closeness in interpersonal relationships, low hostility, and high social support predicted client's ratings of the alliance. Additionally, they found that the therapist's experience was not predictive of the strength of any aspect of the therapeutic relationship.

4. Be active. Research shows that therapists should be active to ensure that clients don't go on doing what doesn't work and they should ensure enough structure in the sessions (Beutler et al., 2004).

5. Ask for feedback. Miller, Hubble, and Duncan (1996) show that good therapists are much likelier to ask for and receive negative feedback about the quality of the work and their contribution to the alliance. The best clinicians, those falling in the top 25% of treatment outcomes, consistently achieve lower scores on standardized alliance measures at the outset of therapy – perhaps because they are more persistent or are more believable when assuring clients that they want honest answers – enabling them to address potential problems in the working relationship. Median therapists, by contrast, commonly receive negative feedback later in treatment, at a time when clients have already disengaged and are at heightened risk for dropping out.

6. Adjust to your clients. Most aspects of the style of therapists are strongly dependent on whether they adjusts to the preferences, hopes, and characteristics of their clients. Flexibility and building *rapport* are essential qualities for good therapists. What specific responses from therapists are responsible for a positive *alliance* varies from client to client. Good therapists are sensitive to the reactions of their clients and can adjust their interactions on the basis of this feedback (Duncan, Miller, & Sparks, 2004).

7. Give compliments. This not only contributes to the alliance, but also ensures that the treatment outcome is 30% more successful than treat-

ments where no compliments are given (Arts, Hoogduin, Keijsers, Severeijnen, & Schaap, 1994).

Shanfield, Matthews, and Hetherly (1993) looked at the differences between good and bad supervisors. Experienced supervisors on the basis of video recordings of their supervision sessions rated colleague-supervisors. They found that good supervisors give enough room to supervisees to develop themselves and are consistent in their supervision style. Less good or even bad supervisors follow their own path and teach rather than focus on the development of the supervisees. They only concentrate on the problems of the supervisees' clients and not on what the supervisees find useful or are concerned about.

Anderson, Schlossberg, and Rigazio-DiGilio (2000) asked supervisees to assess their supervisors. They asked them what their best and worst supervision experience had been. The supervisees rated their supervisors as positive when they showed attention for their personal growth and technical skills. Supervisors who were only concerned with teaching technical skills, however, received negative reviews.

Twenty-Two Applications for Reflection

In the following section you find 22 further ways to apply reflection to your work. Some applications require little time while others may require more extensive concentration. It's nice to vary these, to find out which applications work best and fit yourself as a supervisor and which fit your supervisees. All the applications are of course also suitable for colleagues in peer supervision.

1. Reflecting Team

The supervisees sit in a circle and take turns talking about one of their clients. Each presenter's case is discussed according to a protocol. Roughly 20 minutes are allotted to each case. In addition to the presenter, there is a discussion leader, who is seated outside the circle and, acting as a director, does not participate. The others are the reflecting team. This collegial input often has a positive effect on how the team functions, as participants are able to familiarize themselves with each other's expertise. The maximum size of the group is eight people. The model (Norman, 2003) has clear steps and is somewhat rigid. However, the presenters often derive much benefit from the clarifying questions as well as the affirmations, which they may receive with a Thank you. The steps are as follows:

- *Preparation.* Everyone thinks of a case to introduce. The first supervisee is asked to present his or her case;

- *Presentation.* The first presenter briefly describes his or her case and specifies what he or she would like help with. The others listen without interrupting;
- *Clarification.* The group members take turns asking one clarifying question and one follow-up question (*what, where, when, who,* and *how* questions; preferably no *why* questions). Everyone remains silent until it's his or her turn;
- *Affirmation.* Taking turns, each group member discusses what about the supervisee he or she is most impressed by in the described situation. The supervisee remains silent (except to say thank you);
- *Reflection.* Anything that seems relevant can be shared: technical guidance, suggestions, contemplation, metaphors, poetry, associations, and so forth. Sometimes someone offers a reflection prompted by an earlier reflection. Each group member says one thing or skips his or her turn if nothing comes to mind;
- *Conclusion.* The presenter talks about what most appealed to him or her in the discussion, what seemed applicable, and what he or he is planning to do.

A variant of the *reflecting team* – in this instance the first part is problem-oriented; the latter more solution-oriented – is described by Van Dam (2010). The abbreviated steps of this supervision model are as follows:

Step 1: The supervisee poses his or her question regarding the case.
- What is your question and why you want to discuss it?
- How does this question hamper you during your work?
- Which solutions are not working for you?
- What do you want to do differently?
- What have you already learned about your question?
- What is the worst thing that could happen if your question is not answered?
- What rating would you give the negative impact of this question on your work, on a scale of 0–10, where 10 means the most negative impact and 0 the least negative? How is it that you are at this point on the scale?
- Which aspect of the question do you want the reflecting team to keep discussing?

Step 2: The reflecting team calls for reflections on the presenter's question.
- What has our colleague already done to find an answer to his or her question?
- What different perspective on the question can I offer?
- What could our colleague do to find an answer to his or her question?

Step 3: The interviewer poses questions to the presenter of the case.
- What in the discussion appeals to you and how could this help you?
- What do you need to turn this reflection into a solution?
- How does this solution resolve your question?
- Who or what can be of help to you?
- What does that situation look like?
- What is the first difference you will notice if you apply this solution and what do you have to do to apply that solution?
- Where will this solution bring you, on the scale of 0–10 (see Step 1)?
- What will you do differently from previous situations?
- What do you need to move forward?
- How will your colleagues notice that you have applied this solution?
- When can you apply the solution?

Step 4: Each participant reflects on the supervision session.
- What have you learned during this session?
- How can you use it? Where and when?
- Who or what may help you?
- Which question from the interviewer was most helpful for the presenter of the case on the way to his or her solution?

2. Write a Life Summary

Invite the supervisees to write a short description of how they would like to have their life relayed to their grandchildren (or a young child whom they care about). A few days later, ask them to review the summary and take stock of what is missing in their life and the changes that would be necessary to make the summary a reality.

3. Write a Letter From Your Future

Invite supervisees to write a letter from the future to their current self. Ask them to choose a time in the future that is relevant to them (e.g., 1 year, 5 years). Have their future self from that period of time write to their current self that they are doing well, where they are, and what they are doing. Ask them to provide a description of the most important things that they have done to get to that point. Finally, ask them to offer themselves a wise and kind piece of advice from the future.

> ### Case 18 Letter From Your Future
>
> In my capacity as a trainer of the Mental Health Team of Doctors Without Borders, I coached counselors in northern Sri Lanka. The counselors were working in the refugee camps that were established during the war between the Tamil Tigers and the Sri Lankan government. As part of the training, counselors wrote themselves letters from their future. One of the counselors began to cry as she was writing. Afterward, she said that writing the letter made her realize that she had to continue to take care of her children even though her husband was missing and her house had been set on fire a month earlier. "I felt dead inside. Writing this letter makes me feel alive again," she said.

4. Take Away

Help supervisees to describe five things or ideas that they may use at work, which will let them know that the supervision was worth their effort/time/money. When this exercise is done in pairs, after 5–10 minutes let the supervisees change roles in interviewing each other. This may be done at the end of the entire supervision, or at the end of each session or after a few sessions. Formulating aloud what has been useful and will be taken away from the session helps to better remember these five things or ideas (see *capitalizing*, Chapter 2).

5. Reflection on *Performance*

Invite the supervisees to do this application by themselves or in pairs or triplets. Ask these questions or interview the other(s) using the following questions:

- When did you really feel good about your work?
- Remember as many details as possible about that time;
- What factors made sure that you were satisfied?
- What exactly did you do that contributed to the success?
- What personal qualities did you bring which contributed to the success?

6. Positive Reminiscence

The essence of positive reminiscence is to spend time recalling a positive event from the past. This could be an experience that brings forth pleasant memories, such as a birthday, wedding, a job interview, or a time when you accomplished something important in your life. Supervisees might find benefit in doing this exercise with physical memorabilia – photo albums, trinkets collected from a vacation, trophies or awards, meaningful letters or printed e-mails, or college degrees. After recalling the event, ask supervisees to take a few minutes to simply bask in the past success and pleasant feelings this experience brings forth in them. This experience of stretching out and extending a moment is one example of savoring. Ask them to bring their attention to the details and their positive emotions. Ask them not to analyze the experience: ask them to not pick apart the experience and try to figure out why certain things happened; this is often counterproductive with positive experiences and is not truly savoring. Instead, ask them to focus on the replaying of the experience. This exercise has been shown to build positive emotions and build confidence.

Exercise 26 Defining Moments

This *defining moments* exercise builds on research on the *You at your best* exercise (see Chapter 4). The purpose of this exercise is to facilitate exploration of the supervisees' character strengths, to build a bridge between past crucial experiences and future possibilities, and to link positive identity formation with their character strengths. There are three steps:
1. Ask supervisees to name the defining moment and tell the story (e.g., passing an important exam);
2. Ask them to list the character strengths involved in their story;
3. Ask them to reflect on how this story has shaped how they are (their identity); and how has it impacted them to the present day.

---

7. Savor Your Day

Invite supervisees for 2–3 minutes to reflect on two pleasurable experiences or moments which happened during their day. Ask them to allow/make the pleasure last as long as possible. This savoring taps into the intensification or elongation of positive emotions through focused attention on the present moment. Maybe you know this quote: *"Yesterday is history, tomorrow a mystery, today is a gift, that's why we call it the present."*

8. Sit on Three Chairs

During a supervision session three chairs are placed in a row and supervisees are invited to take turns in sitting in the three chairs and talk about themselves. The first chair stands for their life two years ago, the second seat for their present life, and the third chair represents their life in two years time. Instead of two years one can choose another time frame, such as six months, a year or five or ten years. The others may pose the following questions regarding the time frame associated with each chair:

- How are you doing?
- What is making you happy or satisfied?
- How are you managing to achieve that?
- What would you like to be different?
- What is working for you at this time?
- What will be the next sign of progress?
- What will be your (small) next step?

It goes without saying that the creativity of the participants may provide many more beautiful questions. What's nice about this exercise is that participants look both forward and backwards in reflecting on their life and work.

9. Reflect on Qualities

Everyone has certain qualities. Invite supervisees to take the Values in Action (VIA) Survey of Character Strengths (see Chapter 4) and find out how they can apply their signature strengths as much as possible in their work and private life. When they use those qualities as much as possible flow and well-being will definitely increase.

10. Pay Attention to What Is Going Well

Invite supervisees to observe in the next weeks everything that is going well at work, what doesn't need to change because they are doing the right things. What did they do that was helpful to achieve these things? Also invite them to observe what others, like their colleagues, do well and how they achieve that. What might be useful for the supervisees?

11. Turn on Positivity

We all have the power to turn positivity on and off for ourselves. Invite supervisees to experiment with this and turn positivity on right now. Say: "Take a moment to notice your physical surroundings. Whether you are in your living room, bathroom, on the bus or train and ask yourself: What is right about my current circumstances? What makes me lucky to be here? What aspect of my current situation might I view as a gift to be treasured? How does it benefit me or others? Taking time to think in this manner can ignite the inner glow of gratitude. Take a few moments to savor and enjoy the good feeling you have created for yourself.

Now turn positivity off. Positivity spoiling questions are: What is wrong here? What is bothering me? What should be different and better? Who is to blame?"

Try asking yourself these kinds of questions and follow the chain of thoughts they produce and how quickly your positivity plummets.

Source: Fredrickson (2009)

12. Tell Each Other Positive Events

For this application, invite supervisees to choose someone they like and whom they meet regularly, e.g., a good colleague or their partner. Ask them to arrange with that person to tell each other daily about one or more positive events (at work) of that day for a week (or longer if they would like). This is called *capitalizing* (see Chapter 2). This application will be most effective for their relationship and themselves when the other's reaction is positive and enthusiastic.

13. Three Questions for a Happy Life

Here are three questions which will help supervisees to create a happy life:
1. What did I do today that I found satisfying?
2. What did someone else do that I found satisfying? Did I react in a way so this person might do this again?
3. What else do I see, hear, feel, smell, or taste for which I am grateful?

14. Be Grateful

Invite supervisees to start a journal and write every day about the things for which they are grateful. These may be big things but could also be small everyday things. For instance, just now my daughter offered me a cup of delicious tea. Ask them to also write briefly about why they think these good things happen to them. This way they develop an eye for what precedes these good things and what they say about them. To keep this experience fresh supervisees may choose not to do this every day, but only a few days every week.

Some time ago I walked through San Francisco looking for a restaurant. My eye fell on a restaurant in the Bay Area with the name "Gratitude." "What are you grateful for?" was written in large luminous letters on a sign on the restaurant wall. A nice question to ponder when you want to have dinner somewhere.

15. Change Nongrateful Thoughts

Miller (1995) describes a four-step cognitive-behavioral program to create more gratitude in one's life. Research showed that by following this program you will experience more satisfaction and greater well-being. The four steps for supervisees are as follows:
- Notice your nongrateful thoughts;
- Formulate grateful thoughts instead;
- Replace the nongrateful thoughts by grateful thoughts;
- Convert the positive inner feeling into action: do something with it.

16. Experience Flow

Invite supervisees to think of a moment at work (or in another situation) when they experienced flow. Flow refers to an optimal mental state in which you are completely absorbed in your pursuits; you forget about the notion of time. It is characterized by targeted energy and activity and full involvement, in conjunction with the successful completion/realization of your activities. The main theorist behind this concept is Csikszentmihalyi (1990), together with Seligman the cofounder of positive psychology (PP).

If you experience flow, you feel challenged and fully use your abilities. You can experience flow in almost any situation, and depending on your history and circumstances, almost everyone can also experience boredom or anxiety. The subjective experience of the challenge and the individual set of skills brought to bear determine the quality of the experience. Attention plays an important role, both in obtaining and maintaining flow. Some activities are structured in a way that it is easier to obtain flow, such as sports and games. The features for flow are often there without saying. Flow can also be achieved by controlling your thinking, as in meditation or prayer. Identify those activities which you like, are good at and consider to be a challenge, because these are the most likely opportunities for you to experience flow (Bannink, 2009a, 2012a)

17. Check What You Are Proud of

Invite supervisees to check what they are proud of. Pride might be the opposite of guilt. You are *guilty* of something good instead of something bad. Pride is often looked at with mixed feelings: e.g., in our Dutch culture it is frowned upon when one expresses pride in something he or she did. Feeling proud is the good feeling you get when you optimized a psychological rapport or when your supervisee or client leaves the session satisfied. Pride is also of social importance, because you usually like to share it with others when you are proud. You expect that they also will appreciate your success. Research showed that people who are proud persevere longer with a daunting task than people who do not feel proud (Williams & DeSteno, 2008).

Case 19 Pride

Two years after concluding supervision I came across my supervisee at a conference. He told me the following story. On the way home after the last session he was thinking about how he could apply what he had learned when at home. He came up with an idea and since that time, each night when he puts his three children to bed, he asks them what made them proud that day. It is now a daily ritual in which the children also ask him what he was proud of. If he forgets their ritual, the children remind him: "Daddy, we haven't talked about what we are proud of." He added that this ritual keeps him alert during the day with "What can I tell my children this evening?" When nothing comes to mind that makes him proud that day, he uses the opportunity to do something about it.

18. View the Problem From the Perspective of a Different Job

It is a nice exercise to view the supervisees' problem and the possible solutions from a different point of view. Not from the viewpoint of the therapist, supervisor, or coach, but from the perspective of a different job. Invite supervisees to first choose another job (e.g., the job they wanted to have as a child). One can also work with cards, on which a number of professions are already written. Once the new job is selected everyone is invited to look first at the problem and then at solutions from the viewpoint of their new job. The creativity and new perspectives that this application produces is surprising.

19. Use All Modalities

Invite supervisees to think of a problem; they don't have to tell what the problem is or give any details. Then the supervisor (and other supervisees if present) ask the problem-holder questions such as: "Assume the problem has a shape, what shape is it?"; "What color does the problem have?"; "How does the problem sound?"; "How does the problem feel?"; "What is the smell of the problem?"; "What is the taste?"; "How does the problem move?"

Then the supervisees describing the problem are invited to apply the same modalities to what they want to have instead of the problem. This application often produces surprising results while it is safe for the supervisees because they don't have to tell what the problem is. At follow-up the supervisees are interviewed to tell what is better or has changed since they presented the problem.

Case 20 **All Modalities**

A supervisee in group supervision is invited to concentrate on the problem which she wishes to discuss. She doesn't tell what the problem is. The other supervisees and supervisor ask her questions like those mentioned above such as: "What shape is the problem?"; "What color?"; "How does it feel if you touch it?"; "What sound does it make?"; "How does it smell?"; "How does it taste?"; "What kind of movements does it make?" The supervisee tells them that the problem has taken the form of an elephant and that it sounds like a male voice humming. Then the supervisee answers the same questions about the solutions: what shape is the solution, and so on.

The supervisor ends this exercise by asking the supervisee to observe what happens to the problem and/or the solutions between this supervision session and the next, so she can talk about it when they meet again. The next session she tells them that the elephant started to move and that the sound is now that of a little elf. On a scale of 10–0, where 10 means the problem is gone and 0 means the opposite, the supervisee estimates herself now being at 6; whereas in the first session she was at 3. She doesn't yet know what the solution is going to look like exactly, but she says that it feels that the solution is getting closer and already the problem weighs less heavily.

20. Three Blessings

Invite supervisees to write down each day for a week three good things which happened that day. This is called the *three blessings exercise*. Research within PP has shown that people will be happier and less depressed (up to six months later), even though they perform this exercise for only a week. Both 'normal' and depressed people benefit from this exercise. Next to each positive event, ask them to write about how it was that this good thing happened and what they did to influence these events.

21. What Went Well and What Could Be Better

This is an exercise for supervisees in five steps using the following questions in connection with a challenge:

1. What went well?
2. What didn't go well or could be better?
3. What would you like to do instead?
4. What indications do you have that you can actually show this behavior?
5. What indications do the others have that you can actually show this behavior?

22. Reflect on Group Functioning

It pays off to reflect occasionally on the functioning of the supervision group. The following questions may be helpful:

- If 10 stands for the optimal functioning of our group and 0 stands for the opposite, where do I think our group stands today?
- How is it that the functioning is at this point on the scale and not lower?
- What do we want to keep as it is and doesn't need to change?
- At what point on the scale would I like our group to be in the future?
- How will one point higher look? What will we be doing differently or better?
- What will be signs of further progress?
- How can we get a higher point on the scale?
- Who will do what and when to make that happen?
- How are we going to celebrate progress?

Another way to reflect on the functioning of the supervision group is to use the Group Rating Scale (GRS), which may be filled out at the end of each meeting.

Feedback by the Supervisees

Conventional wisdom suggests that competence engenders effectiveness. As a result there is a continuing education requirement for therapists. But research shows that there is no or little relationship between the experience level and effectiveness with clients (Clement, 1994). So far there is no evidence showing a relationship between supervision and more effectiveness either (Veeninga. 2008; Veeninga & Hafkenscheid, 2010).

The data indicate that increasing the amount and type of training and experience that most professionals receive may even lessen their effectiveness! Researchers distinguished successfully between least and most effective therapists (as determined by outcome, Hiatt & Hargrave, 1995). They found that therapists in the low-effectiveness group tended to have been in practice for more years that those in the high-effectiveness group. They also found that the ineffective therapists were unaware that they were ineffective. Even worse, they considered themselves as effective as the truly helpful therapists in the study!

It is therefore very important that the competencies of professionals are not only assessed by those professionals, but first and foremost by their clients. Miller, Duncan, and Hubble (1997) state that using client feedback to inform the professional would invite clients to be full and equal partners in all aspects of therapy. Giving clients the perspective of being in the driver's seat instead of at the back of the bus may also enable them to gain confidence that a positive outcome is just down the road. "Systematic assessment of the client's perceptions of progress and fit are important, so the clinician can empirically tailor the therapy to the client's needs and characteristics."

They developed the Session Rating Scale (SRS). The SRS is a feedback instrument, divided into the three areas that decades of research have shown to be the qualities of change-producing relationships: (1) the relationship between therapist and client (the alliance), (2) the goals and topics, and (3) the approach or method (the allegiance). Clients are asked to place a mark on each 10 cm line, where low estimates are represented to the left and high to the right. The instruction is as follows: Please rate today's session by placing a mark on the line nearest to the description that best fits your experience.

Each line has a potential of ten marks, with a possible grand total of 40. A centimeter ruler can be used to measure the mark of the client on each line and then you can add them up. There is no specific cut-off score between relationships that have *good* or *bad* change potential. Higher scores (above 30) reflect relationships that have better change potential, lower scores suggest the relationship may need some extra attention. In this case, it is the therapist who should ask: What should I (in my work as a therapist) do differently next time so you (the client(s)) will give higher marks on the scale. The SRS is an engagement instrument, its opens space for the client's voice about the alliance. Duncan (2005, p. 183) states: "Monitoring progress is essential and dramatically improves the chances of success. You don't really need the perfect approach as much as you need to know whether your plan is working – and if it is not, how to quickly adjust your strategy to maximize the possibility of improvement."

Clients whose therapists had access to progress information, like the SRS, were less likely to get worse with treatment and were twice as likely to achieve a clinically significant change. Nothing else in the history of psychotherapy has been shown to increase effectiveness this much!

The SRS can be found in Appendix 6 and at www.scottdmiller.com. There is also a SRS available for children with emoticons; and for use in (peer) supervision there is the Group Session Rating Scale available (GSRS). The SRS has been translated to many languages. When you register on their website, you get all scales free and information on how to use them.

> **"** In supervision we often talked about the effect of the use of the Session Rating Scale. By filling out the SRS myself, I really experienced what exactly this effect is. At the start it is strange when a supervisor asks you to provide feedback on the supervision. Also the question: 'What can I do differently or better next time to get a higher point on the scale?' was unfamiliar. The first time

I didn't dare to say what that might be. The next time, however, I did give feedback and it turned out to be very nice. By doing so we worked more focused on my goals and I got more out of the supervision. It also gives me a good feeling that the supervisor asks me what I want and how I want it. This influences our working relationship in a positive way. 🙶🙶

What is true for therapists and their clients also applies to supervisors and their supervisees: in my opinion these are parallel processes. I always invite supervisees at the end of each session to complete the SRS. They like it; it is extremely effective and hardly takes any time. As their supervisor, even when I receive high scores, I ask what I can do differently or better the next session to get (even) higher scores. And if the supervisees give the highest score possible (total score 40), I ask what I should continue to do in order to maintain these high scores. Please note: this question differs from the (more problem-focused) question what the supervisees should do differently or what we together should do differently.

In the description of *super-supervisors* earlier in this chapter, we saw that asking for feedback from supervisees helps to improve mediocre supervisors to become part of the category of super-supervisors. Also Veeninga (2008, p. 371) states that asking for feedback is a valuable addition to the self-reflection of the supervisor, who can be hindered by blind spots and avoidance tendencies:

> I mean that the supervisee learns to ask for feedback from his client and that the supervisor does the same thing to the supervisee. Learning to give and ask for feedback is considered a basic social skill in CBT; this may in time adjust dysfunctional interactions ... With such simple tools not only is personal supervision appropriately designed, but a picture of the competencies of the supervisor is also provided. In addition, it can contribute to solving disagreements and conflicts that may occur in supervision relationships.

Summary

- Pillar 4 involves reflection by both supervisors and supervisees.
- Some supervisors and supervisees do better than others. Research findings explain these differences, allowing *super-supervisors* and *super-supervisees* to exist.
- There are 22 applications describing ways for reflection.

- Not only reflection by supervisors and supervisees is important; the supervisors should also invite their supervisees to provide feedback using, for example, the Session Rating Scale.
- Asking feedback from their supervisees and showing flexibility in adjusting the supervision to what is important for their supervisees ensures that supervisors grow into the category of *super-supervisors*.

Chapter 7
Follow-Up Sessions

Downward spiral or upward spiral
As I see it, that's your choice.
Barbara Fredrickson

This chapter is about follow-up sessions. Follow-up sessions in positive supervision start with a question about progress: "What is better?" There are four different possible answers to that question, which are described and further explored here. How can supervisors react when they hear that there is no change or that things are even worse since the previous session? The protocol for follow-up sessions is described, followed by practical applications focused on relapse prevention, or more positively: interventions aimed at behavior maintenance. This chapter also deals with the termination of supervision.

Goal of Follow-Up Sessions

According to de Shazer (1994), the goal of the second and each follow-up session is:

- To ask questions about the time between the sessions in such a way that one can definitely discern some progress: If one looks carefully and creatively, one can (virtually) always find improvements.
- To see whether the supervisees feel that what the supervisor and supervisee did in the previous session has been useful and has given them the sense that things are going better.
- To help the supervisees find out what they are doing or what has happened that has led to improvements so that they will know what to do more of or more often.
- To help the supervisees work out whether the improvements have caused things to go well enough that further sessions are not necessary.
- To ensure that the supervisor and supervisee will not do more of what doesn't work, if the supervisees do not see any improvement, and to find a new approach.

The opening question in each follow-up session is about progression: "What is (going) better?" The implicit suggestion of this question is *that* there is something better, and that one only has to look for *what* it is that is going better. This question is different from: "Is anything better?"; "What has been better?"; "What went well?"; "How are you doing?" or "How have you been lately?" Supervisors partially determine, with this opening question about progress, the sort of answer they get.

In the beginning supervisees usually respond with surprise when hearing this question, because they don't expect it. Sometimes they initially respond with "nothing," because they see it that way and don't come up with "something better." Supervisors may then ask very detailed questions about the recent period and search for the moments which were the slightly better or when a particular problem was non or less existent. There are always exceptions to the problem if you look for them; the question is not *whether* those exceptions are present, but *when* they are/were occurring (see Chapter 4).

My experience is that when, as a supervisor, you start the session every time with this predictable opening question supervisees anticipate this and start thinking about the answer prior to the session. In each follow-up session also the four solution-focused basic questions can be used (see Chapter 2). They may be about each session separately ("What are your best hopes for in this session?") or about the entire supervision, or even the whole career or life of the supervisees.

Exercise 27 What Is Better?

Start the next ten or twenty subsequent sessions with the question: "What is better?" Dare to ask that question! As previously mentioned, you will notice that your supervisees start anticipating being asked this and prior to their next session will reflect on what has improved, so they can tell you about this. And if – unfortunately – the answer is that nothing is better or things are even worse, just acknowledge their disappointment, take a look at the possibilities below, and find out how you can stay on a positive track with your supervisees.

De Jong and Berg (2002) developed the acronym *EARS* to distinguish the activities in subsequent sessions. E stands for *eliciting* (drawing out stories about progress and exceptions). A stands for *amplifying*. Supervisees are asked to describe in detail the differences between the moment when the exception takes place and problematic moments. Next, one examines how the exception took place, especially what role the supervisees played in it. R stands for *reinforcing*. The supervisor reinforces the successes and factors that have led to the exceptions through the meticulous exploration of the exceptions and by complimenting the supervisees. And lastly, S, stands for *start again*. The supervisor continues the process with the question: "What else is better?"

Supervisees may provide four different responses to the question as to what is better (Selekman, 1997; Bannink, 2007a,b, 2010b, 2013). How well supervisees are doing and whether the homework suits them determine whether the supervisor should continue on the same path or should do something else. Supervisors must always carefully tailor their questions and homework assignments to the relationship they have with each supervisee (i.e., whether there is a visitor, complainant, or customer relationship). It is important to keep in mind that supervisees want their problem solved, however pessimistic or skeptical they may be. For this reason, it is important to listen closely and to examine *how* they want to change. In subsequent sessions, it is vital to optimize the relationship with the supervisees and to sustain the progress already made and build on it. In addition, one needs to verify whether the homework has been useful and meaningful, and how positive changes may be maintained. The four possible responses are: (1) things are better, (2) we disagree (if there is more than one supervisee), (3) things are the same, and (4) things are worse. The second response is not very likely in supervision, therefore this response will not be addressed in this book any further. For more information on how to react to this response see Bannink (2010b, 2012b, 2013).

When *things are better*, one can generally tell by the supervisee's appearance. They usually look better and often identify many things that have changed. The supervisor enhances the situation by asking for details about the improvements, to emphasize the difference from how things were before, and to pay compliments. Questions for supervisees who report that things are better are:

1. How did you do this?
2. How do you manage to…?
3. How did you manage to take such a big step?
4. How did you come up with that great idea?
5. What did you tell yourself to help you do it that way?
6. What do you have to keep doing so that this will happen more often?
7. How is that different for you?
8. Suppose we see each other again in one month's time. What additional changes will you be able to tell me about then?
9. How do I know that you have enough confidence to halt the supervision now?
10. What ideas do you now have (e.g., about yourself) that are different from the ideas you had before?
11. What would you have to do to go back to square one?
12. Please indicate on a scale of 10 to 0, where 10 means that you completely reached your goal, where you are today?
13. How will you celebrate your victory over the problem?

14. Who will you invite to this party?
15. What will you say in your speech at the party? And who are you going to thank for their support?

At the end of every session, the supervisor asks: "Do you think it's useful for you to return?" If so: "When would you like to return?" The supervisees give feedback using the Session Rating Scale (see Chapter 6).

Homework suggestions for supervisees who report that things are better are:

- Go on doing what works.
- Do more of what works.

Supervisees may feel *that things are the same* and nothing about the situation has changed. In this case, it is useful to find out when small improvements in the situation have been noticeable nonetheless. Supervisees can benefit from every exception that is found by finding ways to make those exceptions happen again. Sometimes remaining stable is a great result in itself; progress is not always attainable.

Questions for supervisees who report that things are the same are:

- How did you manage to remain stable?
- Suppose I were to ask someone who knows you well what is going a little better. What would that person say?
- On a scale of 10–0, how would you rate your current situation?
- What is needed for you to maintain that rating in the days ahead?
- Who among the most important people in your life is most worried about you? Who is the least worried?
- On a scale of 10–0, how worried are those people?
- What would these people say you should do to reach one point higher on the scale?

It may be useful to expand the sessions to include an important person from the supervisee's life to help find solutions to the problem. If the supervisees stay negative and fail to name exceptions, one can ask more competence questions, such as: "How do you cope?"; "How do you manage to go on with these sessions?"

Supervisors may ask themselves the following questions:

- Do we need to revisit the goal?
- Do I have a customer, complainant, or visitor relationship with this supervisee?

Homework suggestions for supervisees who report that things are the same are:

- If the do-something-different task has not yet been assigned, it can be introduced as an experiment, especially if supervisees are stuck in a rut;

The pattern of interaction can be changed through the addition of a new element or through deliberate exaggeration of the pattern;

If supervisees indicate that they cannot exert any control over the problem, they can be asked to *externalize* the problem (see Appendix 5).

Supervisees who say that *things are worse* often have a long history of failure or have contended with big problems for years. If supervisors are too optimistic, they will usually be unable to help them. These supervisees often need a lot of time to tell the story of the problem, including any (negative) experiences with previous professionals. Supervisors may ask *pessimistic* questions when supervisees report that things are worse:

- How do you manage to go on under these circumstances?
- How come you haven't given up by now?
- Could things be worse? How come things aren't worse than they are?

Then usually some more optimistic questions are posed:

- What is the smallest thing you could do to make a minimal difference?
- How can you make the smallest thing happen to a very small extent right now?
- What can others do for you?
- What can you remember about what used to help that you could try again now?
- What would most help you climb back into the saddle and face these difficulties?

It is useful to put these supervisees in an expert-position and ask them, as *consultants*, what their supervision should look like. Questions for expert supervisees are:

- What did supervisors you worked with previously miss?
- Of all the things that these supervisors did, what did you find most disagreeable?
- How could I be of greater assistance?
- What qualities would your ideal supervisor have, and what would he or she do?
- What questions would your ideal supervisor ask you, and what, in your opinion, would be the best course for him or her to follow?
- If I worked with other supervisees who were in the same boat as you, what advice would you give me that would allow me to help them?
- What questions can you think of, that would allow me to help you the most?

Supervisors may ask themselves the following questions:

- Do we need to revisit the goal?

- Do I have a customer, complainant, or visitor relationship with this supervisee?

Homework suggestions for supervisees who report that things are worse:
- It may help to have the exceedingly pessimistic supervisee predict in detail when and how the next crisis will take place. As a result, the crisis may fail to occur or the supervisee may discover better ways to deal with it.
- The supervisee can also be asked to exaggerate the problem. This is a paradoxical assignment. As a result, the gravity of the problem may immediately decrease, as the supervisee doesn't feel like carrying out such an assignment. If supervisees do exaggerate the problem, they will likely experience more control than they first thought they had.
- The supervisor may examine the supervisees' earlier successes in dealing with problems to see what strategies they can try again.

If the supervisor works alone, it may be useful to invite a colleague to sit in and give feedback when dealing with supervisees who say things are worse. With this group of clients, the therapist might also apply the technique of externalizing the problem (see Appendix 5). Lastly, supervisors may discharge themselves in a final rescue attempt if all other strategies have failed. They can explain to the supervisee that they apparently do not understand them or do not have the expertise to help them. They might say it would be best for the supervisee to enlist the help of another supervisor, who may have fresh ideas. Supervisees may agree with this proposition or they may begin to formulate more realistic expectations, after which cooperation may still be possible. For the protocol of follow-up sessions, see Appendix 4.

Exercise 28 Competence Questions

During follow-up sessions focus on what is better or different for your supervisees and how they made that happen. Give them at least three compliments and/or positive character interpretations in the next sessions, and ask questions about their competences, such as: "How did you do that?" or "How did you decide to do that?" Pay attention to the difference this makes for your supervisees and for yourself.

Behavior Maintenance

Orlemans, Eelen, and Hermans (1995) argue that in order to obtain a stable behavioral change, an extrinsic reinforcement should gradually become an intrinsic one. Extrinsic reinforcement means that the reinforcement artificially follows after a certain behavior, while an intrinsic reinforcement is connected naturally with the behavior; the behavior produces satisfactory consequences on its own. Usually, these two reinforcements happen simultaneously. However, it is clear that a purely extrinsic reinforcement provides little guarantee for the sustainability of a particular behavior. When a child plays the trumpet simply because (s)he knows that after the exercise (s)he will receive some candy, this behavior will stay under extrinsic control and will cease when the reward stops. It is often for this reason that well-known, enjoyable melodies are rehearsed early in the learning process to reinforce intrinsically the desired behavior.

Chapter 2 described how positive emotions ensure greater intrinsic motivation to make changes and maintain them, and therefore the task of supervisors is to generate as many positive emotions as possible during supervision. Supervisees are invited during the supervision to think about ways to maintain the benefits from the supervision. In positive supervision one talks rather about *behavior maintenance* than relapse prevention, because this term focuses on gain instead of loss: the term relapse prevention may suggest that relapse is expected.

If things are worse, supervisors should first acknowledge the situation and how supervisees feel about it. However, in positive supervision it is not necessary to elaborate on the causes of the problem. It is more important to invite supervisees to explore how they have been able to get back on the right track in previous situations. And if supervisees still remain upset, supervisors can help them to think about what small steps they may take to get back on track.

Exercise 29 Behavior Maintenance

Inviting your supervisees to make long lists is always a fun and challenging task for them.
- Find 50 good reasons to maintain the positive changes you made;
- Find 50 ways to maintain these positive changes;
- Find 50 positive consequences (for yourself, for important others) of maintaining these positive changes.

If there is discussion about relapse, supervisees are invited to imagine how they, if a relapse should occur, can use their skills to deal with this situation. Research by Snyder (1994) shows that high-hope people are better in finding alternative ways if the original route to the goal is blocked than low-hope people (see Chapter 3). Discussing ways to address possible future problems helps to design alternative solutions, even before these difficulties occur. Using these coping strategies further reduces the risk of relapse.

If relapse happens, it is good to normalize this: progress often takes three steps forward and then again one or two steps back, and it would be a pity to give up both the overall progress and the learning which comes with the backwards steps. One can also suggest a positive label for this journey as relapse does provide the possibility to practice along the way. O'Hanlon (2000, p. 192) states: "If you fall on your face, at least you are heading in the right direction."

There is, however, a more playful way to deal with relapse. Ask supervisees what it takes to get a lower rating on the scale or to get back to square one as soon as possible. This clarifies what supervisees should not do and often gives a lighter feel to the session.

Rothman (2000) found that the decision criteria that lead people to initiate a change in their behavior are different from those that lead them to maintain that behavior. Decisions regarding behavioral change initiation depend on favorable expectations regarding future outcomes, whereas decisions regarding behavioral maintenance depend on perceived satisfaction with achieved outcomes.

Research by Ross and Wilson (2002) shows that recalling an old, pre-change self from the *third-person perspective* helps to deal with the challenge of maintaining personal change. Greater perceived change leads to greater satisfaction with one's efforts thus far and, therefore, make it easier to summon the resources necessary to maintain one's efforts. In sum: psychologically distancing oneself from negative past selves and remaining close to positive past selves promotes well-being.

Questions that may be useful are:

- How did you succeed in making lasting changes in other parts of your life?
- Which of those strategies might be useful now?
- How satisfied are you with the positive changes you made on a scale from 10–0?
- How did you manage to reach that point (how come it is not lower)?
- How will a point higher on the scale look?
- What can you do to get to one point higher on the scale?
- Find supporters to help you in maintaining these changes.
- Whom will you invite? How will you keep them updated? How will you thank them for their help?
- If you look back to your past self, from the perspective of an observer before you made these changes, what would this observer say that is going better in your life right now?
- What would this observer say about you and your qualities?

Concluding Supervision

In positive supervision discussion of concluding the sessions occurs as soon as the supervision starts. This is evident from the questions supervisees receive about goal formulation (see Chapter 3).

- What do you want to have achieved *at the end* of the supervision?
- How can we know when to *stop meeting like this*? (de Shazer, 1991).
- What will be the *best result* for you of this supervision?
- When will you be satisfied with what you have achieved and don't have to come back here anymore?

Who determines the end of supervision? Supervision ends when supervisees think they have reached their goal completely or sufficiently. Often at the start of the supervision a supervision-contract is signed indicating when the supervision will end (see Chapter 9).

Of course supervision may be concluded earlier, for example, if the goal is reached sooner than expected, or concluded later if it takes longer to achieve the goal. Also during the sessions the goal of the supervisees may change and there may be more (or fewer) possibilities than was initially anticipated.

If supervisees are not making progress this should be discussed in a timely manner. When there is a positive alliance between the supervisor and supervisee, the supervisor should do something other than he or she has done so far. If the alliance is not positive after some sessions the supervisor should end the supervision and refer the supervisee to a colleague.

There may be other reasons to stop prematurely, such as the supervisor or supervisee moving to another part of the country, an illness, or a disagreement or conflict between supervisor and supervisee (see Chapter 9). When the goal of the supervisee differs from that of the supervisor (e.g., there is no common goal) there is the risk of a premature ending. If there exists a visitor relationship between the supervisor and the supervisees (see Chapter 8), where they have come involuntarily and can find no goal to work on, the supervision will also end prematurely.

In positive supervision the supervisees determine their goal at the beginning of supervision, and so the supervisor should also accept their declaration that they have sufficiently improved as a reason to end the supervision.

> 66 In this way supervision becomes a positive learning experience, where you are stimulated to want to learn even more and get better at what you are doing. The uncertainty and self-doubt that I experienced at the start of the supervision disappeared and changed into self-efficacy. You grow into a professional who has confidence in herself and the way she functions. In other words,

Sometimes, at the end of the supervision, supervisees bring a bunch of flowers or a nice bottle of wine. This is fine with me, as long as it is something small. At the end of the supervision I also give my supervisees a present as a souvenir. They may choose a copy of my books and, if they so wish, I sign the book with a short personal note. If supervisors are not authors themselves, they may provide a choice of books or give their supervisees a different small gift as a souvenir.

Summary

- The purpose of follow-up sessions is to ask questions about the time between the sessions in such a way that one can discern some progress.
- In follow-up sessions the opening question used by the supervisor partially determines the answer. Possible responses by the supervisees are discussed: "things are better," "things are the same," and "things are worse."
- The protocol for follow-up sessions is described.
- Decision-making about behavior change is different from decision-making about behavior maintenance. Questions about behavior maintenance are presented.
- Concluding supervision may have multiple reasons and is, as much as possible, determined by the supervisees themselves.

Chapter 8
Working
Relationship

If you want to build a ship,
don't drum up people to gather wood,
don't divide the work and give orders,
Instead, teach them to yearn for the vast and endless sea.
Antoine de Saint-Exupéry

In this chapter you find a description of what is known as the working relationship. It is also called the *alliance*. Research shows that this relationship is
very important. Chapter 3 described how an optimal working relationship is
the responsibility of both the supervisor and the supervisee. Using the quote
above as an analogy, in positive supervision supervisors don't divide the work
and give orders, they teach the supervisees to yearn for the endless sea, which
is this case is their job satisfaction and competencies. Using this approach
increases the chances of getting an optimal working relationship.

There are three types of working relationships: a visitor, complainant, and
customer relationship. These three types are explained in this chapter, as well
as the possible reactions of the supervisor and peers in supervision when faced
with the different relationships. A comparison is made with motivational interviewing, Leary's Rose and the stages of behavioral change, used in substance
abuse treatment.

The complainant relationship will be given some extra attention, as it is
usually in this type of relationship between supervisees and their clients where
stagnation and failure occur. However, this type of relationship may also exist
between supervisors and their supervisees or between colleagues in peer
supervision. In these cases it should be established who is willing to change
and how the working relationship can be improved. The difference between
yes, but and *yes, and* is addressed and how both supervisors and supervisees
can benefit from this difference. Finally, this chapter addresses disagreements

and conflicts between supervisors and supervisees and offers a number of tips to both on how to deal with this.

In training courses and in group supervision I love to use the technique of positive gossip. In Chapter 4 a form of positive gossip is described, in which supervisees role-play one of their favorite clients. These clients gossip positively about their therapists (so basically the gossip is about themselves). It is striking that this form of positive gossip almost exclusively deals with the working relationship and rarely with the applied methodology.

Three Types of Working Relationships

Research in psychotherapy shows that the working relationship is important for the outcome of the treatment. Client factors determine 40% of the result, relationship factors 30%, hope and expectation 15%, and methods and techniques only 15% (Duncan, Miller, & Sparks, 2004). Wampold and Bhati (2004) argue that a positive working relationship explains 60% of the therapy success, confidence by professionals in their methodology and in their own techniques 30%, and the technique itself counts for only 10%. It is important to listen to the theory of change of which supervisees use for themselves and to accept their goals as much as possible. Listening to what supervisees think is the key to success will help the supervisors understand what needs to happen and what should be done. It is useful to ask the supervisees how change usually takes place in their life and what works. Since these are parallel processes, these percentages probably also apply to the supervision process.

Bordin (1979, see Chapter 3) mentions the importance of the alliance between the supervisors and their supervisees, where the goal of the supervision, the task for supervisees and supervisors, and the working relationship between them are seen as the three main components.

According to Hawkins and Shohet (2007) supervisors should:

- help supervisees to feel comfortable;
- facilitate and accept feedback from supervisees;
- help supervisees to set clear goals in working with clients;
- encourage supervisees to find new strategies in working with clients; and
- actively involve supervisees in the supervision process.

> " How different was my experience when I met a supervisor for the first time who worked from the solution-focused and positive psychology point of view. I remember well how different the atmosphere was and the attitude of the supervisor in relation to me, the supervisee. I was asked about my goals for the supervision. Soon came up my perfectionism and my fear of rejection. By using a scale of 10–0, we examined how far I already was in completing my goals. I was asked how I was able to give on 6 on the scale instead of a 1 or 0. We examined what competencies I owned and in what situations I managed to act according to my goals. I was surprised: We did not look at my 'weaknesses,' but rather at my skills. I suddenly felt a lot more capable in my work than I previously thought I was. I became even more surprised when the supervisor explained to me what the purpose of supervision is: that you feel competent in your profession and are able to work independently as a psychotherapist. "

The working relationship may be viewed from different perspectives: in this section I address *motivational interviewing* and the *stages of behavioral change* used in substance abuse treatment.

One of the principles of *motivational interviewing* (Miller & Rollnick, 2002) is unconditional acceptance of the client's position. The therapist builds a relationship that is based on collaboration, individual responsibility, and autonomy. Miller and Rollnick state that the necessity of approaching the client in a nonmoralizing way is impeded if the professional is unprepared or unable to defer his own (mistaken) ideas about problem behavior and labels the client's behavior. The therapist reacts with empathy, avoids discussions, and strengthens the clients' self-efficacy.

Miller and Rollnick describe the term *change talk.* This is a method of communication used for enhancing the client's intrinsic motivation to change by stressing the advantages of the behavior change. This change talk assists the client in preparing for change. Regarding methods to elicit change talk, they mention asking questions focused on the future, as is used in solution-focused brief therapy and in positive supervision, such as: "How would you like to see things change?"; "How would you want your life to look in five years time?"; "How would you find the courage to change if you wanted to?" It goes without saying that supervisors should possess the same unconditional acceptance and empathic attitude. The fact that, unfortunately, this is not always the case is described in Chapter 9.

Prochaska, Norcross, and DiClemente (1994) developed a theory about the *stages of behavior change*, which can be broadly compared to the three types of working relationships mentioned above. When a person adopts an indifferent or unknowing attitude ("I have no problem"; the attitude of a client in a visitor relationship), the emphasis is on providing information and on establishing a link between the behaviour to be changed and the worries or problems that others experience. In the next stage, with someone who is contemplating change ("I should change someday"; the attitude of a client in a complainant relationship), the emphasis is on deciding on and initiating the desired behavior. This is followed by the stages of change action (the attitude of a client in a customer relationship), behavior maintenance, and (possibly) relapse (Bannink, 2010b, 2012b, 2013).

Supervisors would do well to adapt their questions, interventions, and (possible) suggestions for homework to the willingness to change of their supervisees. Supervisees will not accept interventions aimed at behavioral change as long as they find that they have no problem to work on and have come on an involuntary basis (visitor relationship) or if they believe that someone else or something else (client, management, health, housing, work, and so on) needs to change (complainant relationship). Supervisors should be skilled in the alignment with the (non)existing willingness to change, not only at the beginning, but during the whole process of supervision. If there exists a customer relationship with a supervisee related to a particular goal, it is possible that a complainant relationship might arise if, for example, supervisors have a different or higher goal that the supervisees and the supervisees are thus no longer motivated to change their behavior.

The importance and effect of giving feedback – by supervisees on the supervisor and supervision using the Session Rating Scale (SRS) – was described in Chapter 6.

Below is an overview of the three types of working relationships and possible reactions of the supervisor or peers in supervision.

In a *visitor relationship* supervisees are mandated. Involuntary supervisees have no problem personally but others have a problem with them or see them as the problem. Naturally this type of supervisees is not motivated to change their behavior. Often the mandated supervisees' goal is to either maintain the relationship with the person or institution referring them or to free themselves from this person or institution as soon as possible.

The supervisor tries to create a climate in which a call for help is made possible. What does the supervisee want to achieve through his or her relationship with the supervisor? What would the person or institution referring them like to see changed in their behavior as a result of the supervision and to what extent are the supervisees prepared to cooperate in this? Here are some tips:

• Assume that the supervisees have good reasons for thinking and behaving in the way they do. Do not be judgmental, and inquire into the perceptions of the supervisees that make their – often defensive – attitude understandable;

- Ask what the supervisees think the person or institution referring them would like to see changed at the end of the supervision;
- Ask the supervisees their opinion on this and what their minimum input might be;
- Ask the supervisees what they want from the supervision (since they are here anyway) and accept their answer.

A visitor relationship between supervisors and supervisees does not exist often. Supervisees usually come on a voluntary basis and have the desire to get better at their work and are willing to change. A customer relationship is created easily. Yet a visitor relationship can emerge. For example, during a training course a supervisee is required to attend supervision because a teacher thinks that the supervisee's performance is inadequate. Or a supervisee visits the compulsory supervision to acquire certain educational points. As long as the supervisee agrees with the referral and is willing to change, there is a customer relationship. If the supervisee disagrees with the conclusion of the former teacher or institution and he doesn't see a problem, there is a visitor relationship. The same applies to a larger group of colleagues who are required to undergo therapy themselves, which they don't consider necessary, to become a member of a specialist association in their field. I come back to this in Chapter 9. If the supervisees acknowledge that there is a problem, but don't show a willingness to change, one speaks of a complainant relationship.

The description of this type of working relationship is listed below.

In a *complainant relationship* the supervisees have a problem and are suffering from it, but they do not see themselves as part of that problem and/or its solutions. They don't feel the need to change their own behavior; they think someone else or something else is to blame for the problem and should change, not the supervisee!

There is no willingness to change and the supervisees would welcome it if someone else would change or the situation would change (e.g., a different manager or fewer administrative duties).

The supervisor acknowledges this situation and asks about their competencies (e.g., "How do you cope?"). The supervisor invites them to talk about exceptions: moments when the problem is or was there to a lesser extent or about the moments when there are already signs of or a small part of what the supervisees want instead of what they don't want. The supervisees are invited to think and talk about their preferred future (without the problem) rather than focusing on the problem and as a homework suggestion may notice when these exceptions occur. This is the difference between *problem-talk* and *solutions-talk* (see Chapter 2).

Roeden and Bannink (2007), Bannink (2010b, 2013), and Den Haan and Bannink (2012) offer many questions for working with persons in a visitor, complainant, and customer relationship.

Case 21 **Complainant Relationship**

During a meeting regarding their clients, held in a mental health institution, the people in the meeting give advice to a colleague about what she should do differently with her client in the therapy. The colleague is tired of these sessions with this client and expresses more and more irritation toward this person. There is a complainant relationship between the colleague and her client, which goes both ways: the client thinks the colleague should solve her problem, whereas the colleague thinks the client shows insufficient effort.

She listens halfheartedly to the advice of her colleagues, because there is also a complainant relationship between herself and her colleagues. "Yes, of course I already tried that a long time ago!" is her response to another suggestion by a colleague, and in this conversation also irritation increases. Because there exists between the colleague and her client and also between the colleagues and the therapist a complainant relationship, there is no use in giving congruent advice. It would have been better if the colleagues had acknowledged how the therapist felt and asked her competence questions first such as: "How do you manage with this client?"; "How are you able to continue when you see so little progress?" Only when there is a customer relationship between the therapist and her colleagues and she is willing to do something else herself in the sessions with her client (she is showing willingness to change to improve the working relationship with her client), may there be an opening to accept the opinions or suggestions from others.

In a *customer relationship* the supervisees see themselves as part of the problem and/or the solutions and are willing to change. In the request for help the word *I* or *we* is present: What can I do to solve this problem? or How can we ensure that we reestablish a good relationship? Customer relationships are not very frequent at the start of psychotherapy; in the case of supervision this will happen more frequently.

However, each position of the supervisees is validated and accepted. The challenge for supervisors is to assess and enhance the supervisees' motivation to change in case of a visitor or complainant relationship. Metcalf (1998, p. 5) states: "If you are not part of the solution, you are part of the problem." This applies to supervisors, supervisees, and clients alike.

Exercise 30 **Caseload**

As a supervisor, assess your working relationship with each supervisee individually. See who of your supervisees may have been referred and may be attending involuntarily. Think about which of your supervisees have indicated that they want to get something out of their sessions with you. Do the supervisees want to achieve something by coming to you or do they think supervision is unnecessary and they just sit there till it is time to leave?

Who, of your supervisees, wants things to change but are not motivated to change their behavior and accept their responsibility?

If the answer to the first question is no, your supervisees have no goal (except maybe that of pleasing or shaking off the person or institution that referred them to you). If your supervisees say someone else is forcing them to come, you have an involuntary supervisee in a visitor relationship. If they think someone else or something else needs to change, you have a supervisee in a complainant relationship.

Adjust your interventions and homework suggestions to your working relationship with every supervisee.

Assessing Motivation to Change

Einstein stated that our theories determine what we observe. Reality is observer-defined and the professional participates in cocreating the system's reality. A psychoanalytical therapist will probably see unsolved conflicts and psychological deficits; a CBT therapist will probably see dysfunctional cognitions and negative schemas. It is impossible for professionals to not have a theory. Supervisors who use positive supervision are also observers and cocreators who help supervisees to write a positive story about their work and lives. There are no definitive explanations for or descriptions of reality. Professionals mustn't be too wedded to the models that they most prefer. Chartier (1938), a French philosopher, stated: "There is nothing more dangerous than an idea when it is the only one you have."

From a social constructivist point of view reality is constructed by the observer, who participates in cocreating the reality; the professional is not an observer on the sidelines. If someone is not motivated to change, the term *resistance* is frequently used. However, this is not a useful concept, because this implies that this person does not want to change and that the professional is removed from the person. It is better to approach this person from a position of cooperation than from a position of resistance, power, and control. "Clients are always cooperating. They are showing you they think change takes place. As we understand their thinking and act accordingly, cooperation is inevitable" (Walter & Peller, 1992, p. 200).

The idea that professionals know what is best for their clients stems from the medical model. If a client in psychotherapy or coaching puts aside the ideas of the expert or does not follow advice, this is usually attributed to the personal or character flaws of that client or to deep-seated pathology. In the medical model, it is expected that the doctor as an expert makes the client better by his interventions. If successful, the doctor can feel competent and gets the credit for the progress. If there is no progress, the blame for the lack of it is sometimes put on the shoulders of the client. That permits professionals to distance themselves from their responsibility.

De Shazer (1984) states that what we as psychotherapists see as signs of resistance are in fact the unique ways in which our clients choose to cooperate. Clients who do not do the homework are not resisting, but cooperating by indicating that this homework doesn't fit in their way of doing things. They are showing the therapist how they think change takes place. If therapists see resistance in the other person, they cannot see their efforts to cooperate; if, on the other hand, they see their unique way of cooperating, they cannot see their resistance.

de Shazer (1984) uses the metaphor of a tennis team:

> With resistance as a central concept, therapist and client are like opposing tennis players. They are engaged in fighting against each other, and the therapist needs to win in order for therapy to succeed. With cooperating as a central concept, therapist and client are like tennis players on the same side of the net. Cooperating is a necessity, although sometimes it becomes necessary to fight alongside your partner so that you can cooperatively defeat your mutual opponent. (p. 85)

Supervisors take part in the game and they should play on the same side of the net with their supervisees instead of playing on the opposite side. The problem then becomes the opponent of both. This vision is derived from *narrative therapy,* where the intervention of externalizing the problem is frequently used (see Chapter 5).

66 Not just the working relationship with the clients, but also the working relationship with the environment of these youngsters is an important topic in the supervision. You may have a customer relationship with a youngster, but this may not be the case with the group leaders of the institutions these youngsters live in. By first focusing in positive supervision and then in psychotherapies on these topics, I notice that my clients are more motivated. They work on their own goals and the best part is that they themselves come up with great ideas of how they want to achieve those goals and what they need to do to get there. 99

Using Leary's Rose is another way of looking at the working relationship. Problems between people are primarily determined by how individuals respond to each other. Leary (1957) developed a practical model to categorize social relationships. He distinguishes two main dimensions: one dimension which makes up the vertical axis is power and influence. The existence of power and influence is characterized by the word *above* and the lack of this uses the word *below*. The second dimension which becomes the horizontal axis is based on personal proximity and sympathy. When one has this it is labeled *together* and when this doesn't exist and there is distance and this is called *opposed*. These two dimensions govern how people – including supervisors and supervisees – interact with each other. People with a great need for power position themselves above others. They are quick to engage in battle and tell others what they have to do. People at the other end of the power spectrum take a subservient or dependent position. If the division of influence is equal, the relationship is symmetrical. If it is unequal, the relationship is complementary. Some people only feel happy if they can work with others. Cooperative behavior, such as providing support and help, suits them. People at the other end of the spectrum are associated with behavior that creates distance and implies opposition.

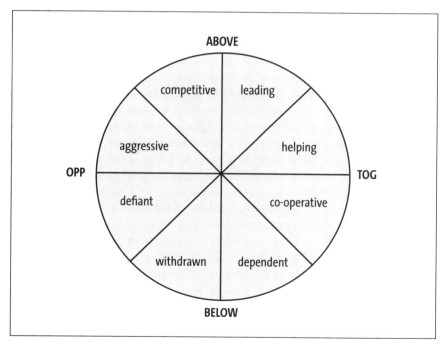

Figure 2. Leary's Rose

On the basis of these dimensions, Leary came up with four communication positions: *below and together*, *above and together*, *below and opposed*, and *above and opposed*. People often assume a preferred position within one of these four quadrants. There may also be a varying preference for two (or more) quadrants. The communication position taken by one person prompts in the other person a supplemental (complementary) or an opposite (symmetrical) interactional position: Above elicits below, below creates above, together invites opposed, and opposed provokes together. Communication behavior and, hence, interactional disruptions proceed according to these rules.

In problem-focused supervision, the supervisors usually adopt the *above and together* position (they are the expert), which automatically puts the supervisees in the *below and together* (or opposed) position. The supervisor is leading and helping and the supervisee is cooperating and following. Only at the end of the supervision the supervisees adopt a more equal role. But if supervisors adopt the above and together position, there is the risk of putting their supervisees in the above and opposed position or in the below and opposed position. In those cases the supervisors speak of resistance or noncompliance, because the supervisees are not doing what the supervisors want them to do.

In positive supervision, the supervisors usually adopt the *below and together* position, which causes the supervisees to move, seemingly automatically, to the *above and together* position, in which they are seen as coexperts from the start. They often already possess the solutions without sometimes knowing it. Inquiring about supervisees' ideas, talents, ambitions, and competencies produces equal cooperation between the therapist and clients.

Supervisees with whom there is a customer relationship are in the together position; supervisees with whom there is a complainant relationship are in the opposed position as far as behavior change is concerned. If the supervisors notice themselves becoming irritated, insecure, or discouraged, there is *countertransference*, that is, a negative reaction by the supervisor to the supervisees behavior. Acknowledging the problem and inviting supervisees to talk about previous successes and competencies is helpful to invite supervisees to adopt a together position. Also inquiring about their good reasons not to change at this point in time may be helpful.

Exercise 31 Leary's Rose

Find out which position in Leary's Rose is your favorite one to assume as a supervisor and when you have succeeded in discovering this – if you wish to do so and maybe only temporarily– adopt another position. What differences do you notice with regard to yourself and also for your supervisees?

"The strict hierarchy with its focus on errors disappears; there is a more equal relationship, in which you both bandy thoughts around about certain issues and possible solutions. Because there is also room for the person of the supervisee you feel recognized and respected. Personal circumstances or characteristics that complicate working with clients are addressed, so that you feel free to work properly."

Case 22 Leary's Rose

A problem-focused supervisor gives advice to his supervisee on how to interact with a difficult client. Thus the supervisor positions himself in the above-together segment in Leary's Rose. He says: "Your client should do her homework, otherwise your therapy with her is going to be a failure." The supervisee has little confidence that this is the right way forward (of course he knows the client better than the supervisor), but dare not say this out loud. In addition, he has already spoken with his client about her forgetfulness to do her homework and this didn't have the desired effect. In problem-oriented supervision, in which the supervisor is the expert and gives advice, there is the risk that the supervisee will react with *yes but*.

In positive supervision, however, supervisors will ask the supervisees themselves what good ideas they have to deal with such clients (inviting supervisees to take the above-together position) and what works or has worked for this client.

Chapter 2 described how positive supervision is not problem-phobic. If supervisees like receiving tips and advice, the supervisors should first ask them what good ideas they themselves have and what has worked already, even if only a little bit. After that, the supervisors could give – preferably on invitation only – their advice. Supervisees are first invited as it were to open their own store of ideas and competencies; and only later on would the supervisors open their own personal store and offer suggestions or even some advice if needed.

"The acknowledgment of how difficult some situations are helps me to continue with a complex case, strengthens the idea that I am on the right track and helps me getting new bright ideas. I am often surprised by the simplicity of the solutions. It often turns out to be easy to generate and implement new ideas and interventions."

Strategies in a Complainant Relationship

Walter and Peller (1992) describe four strategies that may be applied with supervisees who do not see themselves as being part of the problem and/or the solution which means there exists a complainant relationship with them. My experience is that in particular the second strategy is very helpful.

1. "I wish I could help you with this, but I am not a magician. I do not think that anyone is able to change anyone else. How else might I help you? Or In what way is this problem a problem for you?"

2. Investigating the hypothetical solution: "Imagine the other person changing in the direction you desire, what would you notice that was different about him or her? What would you notice that was different about yourself? What difference will this make to your relationship with him or her? When is there a moment when this is already occurring?"

3. Investigating the future if the other is not changing: "What can you still do yourself?"

4. Figuring out the hoped-for outcome behind earlier attempts: "What do you hope to achieve here finally? What will change when the problem is resolved? How do you know that the other person has some responsibility in this situation and not you? How do you manage to not take on that responsibility, even if this is difficult?"

It is understandable that supervisees sometimes have a complainant relationship with their clients. This is often the case when there is stagnation. In a group supervision, I noticed that the supervisees often used terms like hard, difficult and complicated.

In this way the reactions of the others (including the supervisor) are partly determined. The supervisees leaned back; they showed less attention, motivation and enthusiasm in discussing the case. I suggested using terms such as challenging and interesting instead, in order to instill and maintain the curiosity and motivation of the group. It takes some time getting used to these terms, but the effect is soon noticeable. They also start copying the terms with a smile: "I would now like to discuss a very challenging client."

In supervision supervisees state frequently that someone else needs to change and usually this is their client. There is stagnation or the clients are not adhering to their agreements. Supervisees feel irritated, discouraged or uncertain. This is called *countertransference*. In these cases there exists a complainant relationship between the supervisees and their clients, after all: the supervisees think the clients need to change.

There is the risk that supervision addresses only these third persons (the clients), who according to the supervisees should change, and who are not present during the supervision session. This hardly leads to workable solutions. To focus on the supervisees again and what they can and are willing to do to achieve a better working relationship with their clients, the following questions are helpful:

- Suppose your client changes in the way you want them to change, what will you be doing differently? How will your client react differently? And how will you react differently to that?
- A more pessimistic, but sometimes more realistic variation is: "Suppose your client will not change (sufficiently) in the way you want them to change, what can you do differently to ameliorate the situation and your cooperation?"
- What is the goal of your client?
- How is this a problem for you?

Of course supervisees may have a complainant relationship not only with their clients, but also with, for example, their managers or colleagues, or with regard to certain challenging circumstances, such as high production targets.

Many cases presented in supervision relate to clients with whom a complainant relationship exists. I believe that many supervision sessions would become unnecessary when supervisees begin to ask themselves the next question: "Suppose I have a visitor or complainant relationship with this client (instead of a customer relationship, as I supposed), what would I do differently?" This applies to both the interventions during the sessions and the homework suggestions. It is my experience that many supervisees wrongly assume that all their clients are willing to change and therefore use congruent interventions and behavioral tasks.

Students in training courses are often only taught congruent interventions and methodologies (as used in the many protocols in mental health care), which will not work for clients with whom a visitor or complainant relationship exists. Usually customer relationships are only a minority among their clients.

I think more attention should be given in training courses on how to optimize the working relationship between therapist and client and how to motivate clients to change. In this way stagnation, failures, and also burnout among professionals could be prevented.

> ❝ I find it very valuable that positive supervision places so much emphasis on the working relationship. During supervision you learn to pay close attention to the alliance with your clients from the start. In previous supervisions I was not used to paying atten-

tion to the working relationship as having a major influence on deciding which steps you take and don't take in psychotherapy. By consciously paying attention I learned to take different steps when a client doesn't cooperate or when there is stagnation. Earlier on I would have done more of what isn't working by continuing to apply a protocol. 🙲

Case 23 **Motivation to Change**

A supervisee explains that he gets discouraged because his client is not moving forward and, in addition, doesn't follow his suggestions and advice. It's because of this that the supervisee doesn't push hard for results any longer. The supervisor asks if the supervisee is still willing to change himself to improve the working relationship with this client: the question is whether he himself still has a customer relationship with his client. The supervisee is still prepared to make an effort. "How could you improve the relationship with your client?," the supervisor asks. The supervisee decides in the next session to evaluate together with his client what in her life goes well (and doesn't need to change), and to compliment her about this at least three times.

At the next supervision session he says that the atmosphere between him and his client has become a lot better and this has made a difference to him between being reluctant to have a next session and looking forward to it.

If supervisees are no longer willing to do anything themselves to improve the relationship with their clients (e.g., they decide to stay in a complainant relationship), they should terminate the sessions and refer their clients to someone else. Clients have nothing more to gain from these supervisee.

A complainant relationship may exist not only between supervisees and their clients, but also between supervisors and their supervisees or among supervisees. The supervisors may want the supervisees to do something for which the supervisees do not see any need to change. If the supervisees do not perceive a problem and the supervisors do, there is a visitor relationship. Training courses often set out what the competencies of trainees or supervisees should look like. But supervisors and/or supervisees do not always endorse the demands made by training courses or institutions. In those cases there exists also a visitor relationship.

More often, however, complainant relationships exist, where supervisees do have a problem, but don't want to put any effort in changing the situation. In these cases, supervisors or colleagues in peer supervision may pose questions corresponding with a complainant relationship (see earlier this chapter). An important question is whether the supervisors or colleagues in peer supervision are still motivated to change their behavior in an effort to better cooperate with their supervisees or their peers.

Exercise 33 Positive or Negative Emotion

Take a look at your agenda and see what emotions certain names of your clients or supervisees generate. If you get a positive feeling, you are probably looking at the names of clients or supervisees with whom you have a customer relationship. If you get a negative feeling, you are probably looking at the names of clients or supervisees with whom you have a complainant relationship or even a visitor relationship.

Another way to improve the working relationship is to use the *interactional matrix*, frequently used in solution-focused brief therapy *(*SFBT), in which questions from different perspectives are asked. The matrix may also be applied in the event of conflicts (see later this chapter and Appendix 5).

The matrix can be used when there is a complainant relationship between supervisees and their clients, between supervisors and supervisees, or between peers in supervision. Ask supervisees (or yourself as a supervisor) these three questions, using the following sequence:

1. When this problem is solved, what will you notice that is different about the other person? What will you see him/her doing differently? What else?
2. When this problem is solved, what will this other person notice that is different about you? What will this other person see you doing differently?What else?
3. When this problem is solved and you are being watched by an outside observer, what will he/she notice that is different about your relationship with the other person? What will this observer see both of you doing differently? What else?

Earlier in this chapter it was suggested that *countertransference* often exists in complainant relationships. The most common feelings are irritation, discouragement, and uncertainty. Irritation tends to lead the person to hurt, criticize, control, and fight the other; discouragement tends to have them withdraw and to do less; and uncertainty tends to make the individual spoil the other, be too cooperative, avoid, or be too cautious. If these feelings exist, one would do well to find ways to convert these negative emotions and behaviors to positive emotions and behaviors.

If supervisors or supervisees notice that they become irritated, discouraged, or uncertain, there is almost always a visitor or complainant relationship, in which the supervisors wrongly assume their supervisees, or the supervisees wrongly assume their clients, are motivated to change. Again, they should ask themselves if and/or what they themselves might do differently to improve the working relationship.

Yes but and *yes and*

The expression *yes, but* is frequently heard. In reality *yes, but* is simply a form of *no*, it is merely not expressed in a direct way. "Yes, but I see this in a different way" or "Of course you are right, but (you are missing something or you are not seeing the whole picture)." With *yes, but* energy is extracted from the conversation, it soon becomes a discussion about who is right or wrong. People also use *yes,but* when talking to themselves. For example: "Yes I should do more exercises, but right now I don't have the time to do so." This shows that people are contemplating change (see the stages of behavior change, earlier in this chapter), but are not yet ready to take action (there is a complainant relationship regarding to this behavior). *yes, but* ensues a downward spiral of negativity. Therefore it is more beneficial to use *yes, and* to generate more possibilities and better cooperation. Now an upward spiral of positivity is created (see Table 5).

   This also applies to supervisors and colleagues in peer supervision. When they use *yes, but* chances are high that they are themselves in a complainant relationship. Supervisors should – as they are role models for their supervisees – train themselves to use *yes, and* instead of *yes, but*.

Table 5. Differences between *yes, but* and *yes, and*

Yes, but	Yes, and
Excludes or dismisses what precedes it.	Expands and includes what precedes it.
Negates, discounts, or cancels what precedes it.	Acknowledges what precedes it.
Is often perceived as pejorative.	Is often perceived as neutral or positive.
Suggests that the first issue is subordinate to the second issue.	Suggests that there are two equal issues to be addressed.

© Fredrike Bannink

Exercise 34 *Yes, but* or *Yes, and*

Explain the difference between *yes, but* and *yes, and* to your supervisees. Ask someone to make a random announcement (e.g., about the weather or the news) and ask another person to follow up with *yes, but*. A third person does the same, and so on. Let this go on for a couple of minutes; then ask the group whether they are getting anywhere in this manner. You will notice that the discussion goes around in circles and that the members of the group look for ways to convince each other that they are right. The atmosphere will probably turn negative pretty soon.

Now do the same exercise and replace *yes, but* with *yes, and*. After a couple of minutes everyone will notice that the atmosphere is more positive and open and that new themes have come to the fore. The *yes, and* exercise is an excellent technique to show how cooperation can be improved.

Exercise 35 *Yes, and* in a Different Way

This exercise can be done in pairs to discover how *yes, and* builds possibilities and cooperation. The steps are as follows:
- Invite one person to propose an activity, for example, organizing a party or meeting together;
- Ask the second person to respond with: "Yes, what I like about your proposal is..."
- Then the second person makes another proposal: "And then I propose to...."
- The first person replies with: "Yes, what I like about your proposal is..."
- Then the first person makes another proposal: "And then I propose to...."
- This is repeated a couple of times.

Disagreements and Conflicts

While supervision is often highly rated (Veeninga, 2008), there are clear indications that supervision is not always without problems. There are estimates that as many as 40% of supervisions contain disagreements and conflicts (Orlinsky & Ronnestad, 2005). How and whether these are addressed in supervision, in most cases, remains unclear.

Sometimes the supervisees do not function well; sometimes the supervisors do not function well. This may lead to disruption of the supervision and to disagreements and conflicts. Disagreements may also arise when supervisors and supervisees disagree about, for example, the goal of supervision (see Chapter 3), the execution of a particular therapeutic treatment or any other area of work.

If *supervisees* do not function well (enough), the supervisors should signal this and discuss the situation in due time with their supervisees. In positive supervision supervisors will always ask their supervisees how they could be of assistance to help the supervisees function better. If supervisees agree that they are not functioning well and are motivated to change, then there exists a customer relationship between the supervisor and supervisee. If the supervisees agree, but are not willing to change their behavior, or do not have the energy or possibility to change their behavior, then there exists a complainant relationship between them. If the supervisees do not agree and do not see any problem, whereas the supervisors do, there exists a visitor relationship between them. Earlier in this chapter the possibilities to address this are described.

"The subject of nonfunctioning *supervisors* has received little attention so far," according to Beunderman and Van der Maas (2011, p. 84). As a cause of the nonfunctioning they state that supervisors too, besides, for example, psychotherapists, are at risk of emotional and physical problems and burnout. Moskowitz and Rupert (1983) reported that 40% of supervisees experienced conflicts with their supervisor. Unfortunately it is presumed that more supervisees have disagreements and conflicts with their supervisors than was previously thought.

Another cause is perhaps the inability or unwillingness to adapt to what is important for supervisees. More than likely, not all supervisors possess the same level of empathy and unconditional acceptance, and probably equally true is the fact that not all supervisors will work without personal problems or psychological disorders getting in the way. Because it is often not clear how disagreements and conflicts can be addressed, below are some tips for supervisors and for supervisees.

Tips for Supervisors

Many disagreements and conflicts can be prevented or resolved when at the end of each meeting the Session Rating Scale (SRS) is used. The supervisees are invited to give their opinion regarding four areas: (1) working relationship with the supervisor; (2) goals and topics; (3) approach or method; and (4) total rating.

After supervisees have completed the SRS, the supervisors always ask what they can do differently or better, themselves, according to the supervisees, to get a (even) higher rating at the end of the next session. More information about the SRS can be found in Chapter 6.

Case 24 **Fresh Tea**

At the end of a supervision session in a coaching setting my supervisee as usual completes the SRS. He scores the working relationship a 7, the others an 8 or higher. I asked him what I could do differently or better the next session, in order to get a higher score on the working relationship. "Pour me fresh tea," the supervisee replied smiling. I confessed to him that I thought the tea I had poured to someone in the previous hour would still be good enough. The lesson I learned was to always make a fresh pot of tea!

When there is a conflict, both supervisors and supervisees may ask themselves the three questions from the *interactional matrix* (see earlier in this chapter and Appendix 5). The term *problem* is then replaced by the term *conflict* or the less loaded term *issue* while using the following sequence:

- When this issue is solved, what will you notice that is different about the other person? What will you see him/her doing differently? What else?
- When this issue is solved, what will this other person notice that is different about you? What will this other person see you doing differently? What else?
- When this issue is solved and you are being watched by an outside observer, what will he/she notice that is different about your relationship with the other person? What will this observer see both of you doing differently? What else?

If the supervisors and supervisees are not able to resolve the conflict, inviting a neutral – or rather multipartial – mediator is a good idea. This mediator can ask the same three questions listed above to both, followed, for example, by the question where on the scale of 10–0 both are now (10 means the desired situation in the future has been attained and 0 means the opposite). The mediator can also ask how they will make this happen and what will be signs of progress (the four basic solution-focused questions, see Chapter 2). More information about *solution-focused mediation* and *solution-focused conflict management* can be found in Bannink (2006, 2008b, 2009b, 2010a, 2010c).

Sometimes associations, institutions, and companies provide the opportunity to resolve conflicts using, for example, a counselor, a supervisory committee, or board of appeal. A mediation clause may be included as part of the supervision agreement (see Chapter 9).

Tips for Supervisees

It is important that your current supervisors not do the same as their predecessors if what those supervisors did didn't help. Supervisees are competent to inform their supervisors about:

- What was pleasant or annoying about previous supervisions and supervisors?
- What was useful and what wasn't?
- What the present supervisor should not do and what they should definitely do, based on past experience with previous supervisors?

If the supervisors' manner and way of working correspond to the supervisees' ideas about how change takes place and they act in accordance with those ideas, there will always be cooperation. Chapter 3 includes ten tips for optimizing the working relationship. Duncan (2005) suggests six tips for clients who disagree or have conflicts with their therapist in psychotherapy. The same tips probably apply to supervisees in relation to their supervisor:

1. If you do not like your supervisor, find a different one.
2. If you think your supervisor doesn't like you and doesn't understand or appreciate your ideas, find a different one.
3. If you disagree with the supervisor's goals or find that they are not your goals, find a different one.
4. If you disagree with your supervisor's ideas or suggestions or if you do not get what you ask for and your feedback does not make your supervisor change his or her approach, find a different one.
5. If you think that your supervisor views your problem or situation as hopeless or impossible to solve or thinks that it will be years before anything changes, find a different one.
6. If you do not notice anything positive within three to six sessions, you may want to bring it to your supervisor's attention. If no progress is made, find a different one.

Summary

- The working relationship – the alliance – between supervisors and their supervisees, and between supervisees and their clients, is important.
- Three types of working relationships are discussed: the visitor, complainant and customer relationship and how supervisors can optimize these relationships.
- A comparison between the three types of relationships with motivational interviewing, Leary's Rose, and the stages of behavioral change as used in the treatment of substance abuse is described.
- More applications on how to handle a complainant relationship are offered, because this relationship often occurs in cases where there is stagnation or failure. One of the applications to help supervisees making progress is the interactional matrix.
- Resistance is not a useful concept and turns other people into enemies. Therefore, start from the position of cooperation and play on the same side of the tennis net with your supervisees.
- *Yes, and* provides more possibilities and better cooperation than *yes, but*.
- Disagreements and conflicts between supervisors and supervisees are probably more common than was previously thought. A number of tips are given to supervisors and to supervisees to deal with this.

Chapter 9
Important Issues in Positive Supervision

The pessimist sees difficulty in every opportunity.
The optimist sees the opportunity in every difficulty.
Winston Churchill

This chapter describes a number of practical issues, such as how to make a supervision agreement at the start of the supervision process. Also discussed are how to create an agenda, write reports, use audio and video material, do practical exercises during supervision such as role-plays or making drawings, and give homework assignments. Other issues covered are reporting to third parties, supervision via e-mail or Skype, training courses for supervisors, and personal therapy for professionals to enable membership in a specialist psychotherapy association.

Supervision Agreement

Often at the start of the supervision process an agreement is signed between the supervisor and the supervisees. Sometimes such an agreement is even mandatory. In this agreement usually the following items are included:
- The names of the supervisee and supervisor, date of the contract;
- The training course the supervision is part of;
- Agreements on the extent of the supervision, duration per session, making written reports of the session, the costs, the method of payment, how to cancel appointments, reporting to third parties, and so on;
- The goal of the supervision;
- Agreements about evaluating and concluding the supervision; and
- Agreements about how to handle disagreements and conflicts (e.g., a mediation clause).

It is also possible to use such a contract in peer supervision, however, this is less common. For example, an agreement may be signed on the scope and content of the peer supervision, whether there will be a chairperson and how writing reports – often in peer supervision participants take turns – takes place.

Writing Reports

Usually the supervisees write a report of every supervision session. Advantages over just an oral report are that the supervisees, in order to be able to make a report, have to reflect on the last session and that during the next supervision sessions it is easier to come back to what has been said or done.

Some institutions or training courses require written reports. In peer supervision such a report is usually written in turns. In the next session, after the individual chosen has given the report, there is brief feedback on the report and, if necessary, it is supplemented or amended by the others in the group. In positive (peer) supervision the supervisor (and colleagues) compliment the reporter for (the effort of) writing the report.

Creating an Agenda

Usually at the start of the supervision session an agenda, with the items to be discussed, is created. The supervisees usually propose the points to be discussed, but supervisors can add points to the agenda as well, which they, or the institution in which the supervision takes place, find important.

In positive supervision a question about goal formulation is asked prior to every agenda item: "What will be best outcome for you from discussing this item?" or "What is your goal in discussing this item?" This is different from what happens in problem-focused supervision, where no goal formulation is added. The same questions about goal formulation may also be asked about the session itself (see Chapter 3). This is similar to positive *meetings*, where for every agenda item first the goal is stated (Bannink, 2010a, 2012c).

Audio and Video Recordings

It is useful to invite supervisees every now and then to present audio and video recordings of the sessions with their clients, to get a clearer and more complete picture of what they are actually doing in working with their clients.

Usually a clip is viewed together, where the supervisor (or supervisee) freezes a particular moment and discusses what happened in the conversation.

The emphasis is often on what didn't go well and what the supervisee should have done differently. This ensures that reviewing these recordings may sometimes be perceived as threatening.

However, also viewing or hearing these recordings can be done differently. Analogous to certain types of *video-home-training* (a form of family care in which home video recordings are made of problematic situations), excerpts are also (or only) viewed which are satisfactory to the supervisees. The supervisees may, prior to the supervision, edit some successful clips, thus creating a picture of what is going well and what the supervisees do that works. If there are fragments viewed which the supervisees are not happy about, the supervisor can still take a detailed look at what went well, even just a little bit, and discuss what the supervisees may do differently or better next time.

In supervision one can also make use of *video modeling* or *video self-modeling*. *Video modeling* or *video monitoring* uses videos that show how people could behave. It is a form of *observational learning* (Bandura, Ross, & Ross, 1961, in which the desired behavior is taught by first looking at a video demonstration in which someone performs the desired behavior, and the other person then imitates the desired behavior. In *video-self-modeling* (VSM) people see themselves perform the desired behavior on video and then imitate this behavior. VSM is used to learn (social) skills and to improve communication skills or sports performance. It is also used successfully in the treatment of children with autism (Bellini & Akullian, 2007).

Often in supervision recordings are reviewed without first formulating the goal. What does the supervisee want to have achieved at the end of the viewing? What would be the best outcome for the supervisor? Goal formulation is important when watching (or listening to) audio or video material. In positive supervision first the question about goal formulation is asked: "What will be the best outcome for you in viewing/listening to this recording?" or "How will you know this has been helpful to you?"

When the goal formulation is ignored, a discussion of audio or video material often fizzles out in a prolonged evaluation of what did go well or – more often – did not go well. This will not always be the best result for the supervisees (or their supervisor). More information about the importance of goal formulation is described in Chapter 3.

Exercise 36 Best and Worst 10 Minutes

Invite supervisees to show you the best and the worst 10 minutes from a video recording they made. Discuss together, by viewing very precisely, what they have done well and what they could do differently in order to become even more effective. Or just view together the best 10 minutes and skip the worst 10 minutes. Remember: research shows that monkeys (and probably humans too) learn more from their successes than from their failures!

Practical Exercises

During supervision practical exercises are a useful and pleasant alternative to talking about what supervisees do. Think of role playing, making drawings, using metaphors, or making a mind map (see Chapter 5).

In a role-play usually the supervisors model a certain intervention first; the supervisees play the role of their clients. Later on, the role-play may be turned around, with the supervisor playing the role of the client and the supervisees show how they perform the intervention. The role-plays are then discussed afterwards.

In addition to doing role-plays during the session, the supervisees may be invited to play a certain role in-between sessions. Think of the possibility of *counterconditioning*, where supervisees practice a certain behavior that is incompatible with their negative feelings. For example, if a supervisee reports feeling anxious when talking with a dominant client, (s)he practices behavior which is in contradiction to that fear, for example, by sitting more up-straight in the next session with that client, by making more eye contact with the client, talking a little louder, and setting boundaries earlier.

Another form of role-play is the *do-as-if task*, used in SFBT, which is comparable to counterconditioning. Most people assume that they have to wait until a problem is solved before they can behave differently. Instead of waiting until the problem (preferably without too much work) is gone, the supervisees have the opportunity to feel stronger and more in control over the problem *by pretending* the problem is solved. The supervisor invites the supervisees to behave *as-if* things are improving or have improved. This may happen during the session: the supervisees, using role-play, pretend the problem is solved, or act as if they are higher on the scale (closer to their goal) and to pay attention to the differences this makes with the current situation. The do-as-if task can also be given as a homework suggestion. The do-as-if task is a behavioral task and therefore only suitable for supervisees who are motivated to change (with whom there is a customer relationship, see Chapter 8).

Exercise 37 Worst Possible Professional

A funny form of role-play is to ask supervisees to play the *worst possible professional*. This is also known as: "How to fail most successfully." This role-play is safe and often leads to great hilarity. Later on a second role-playing may be done where the supervisees (the same person or other persons in the case of peer supervision) behave in the best possible way.

During a training course I did as a Mental Health Trainer for Doctors Without Borders in Somalia, the medical doctors had great fun showing each other how they could be the worst possible doctors, by being rude and not interested in their patients. They were looking at their phones all the times and did not look at their patients at all. To be sure everyone understood that this was a role-play about being the worst possible professional, they wore a paper vest saying: "bad doctor."

In supervision in addition to talking about their work, scale-walking (see Chapter 5), viewing/listening to audio and video recordings and role-plays, supervisees and their supervisors can make good use of *drawings, mind maps*, and *metaphors*. For example, supervisees are invited to make a drawing, comic strip, or collage of their desired future (their goal), the path to the goal, different steps on the scale, and so on. In Chapter 3 more suggestions are described. The four basic questions, described in Chapter 2, may be put down in four drawings, with a large sheet of paper is folded into quarters and in each box the answer to one of the four basic questions is drawn by the supervisees.

Sometimes supervisees use nice metaphors, such as the supervisee who said that at the end of the supervision that she wanted to be *at the top of the mountain*, or the supervisee who at the conclusion of the supervision wanted *to be in control*. These supervisees can use their metaphors in one or more drawings (e.g., a comic strip).

Supervisees may also individually or in peer supervision create a *mind map* regarding a certain problem and a mind map regarding possible solutions. Everyone is invited to write or draw with colored pencils and felt-tip pens what comes to their mind following something written or drawn by the others in the group. This exercise often produces creative ideas. The supervisees may also make a booklet containing their *success recipes*. In this booklet they collect their successes at work so they can reread them from time to time.

Case 25 **Pippi Longstocking**

A supervisee tells her supervisor that she has trouble making reports. She compares herself to her colleagues whom she thinks are far better and faster at this and she tries to postpone making reports as long as possible. Lately she has been criticized by her manager about her reports, who thinks she is, otherwise, doing fine in the rest of her work. The supervisee often thinks very low of herself and sees herself as being small. This feeling refers to a number of previous moments in her life in which she also felt small and unworthy. The supervisor asks her which image comes to mind when she sees herself as being small and she answers that she thinks of Calimero, a cartoon figure of the 1980s, a black little chicken living in a family with only yellow chicks. Calimero always said: "They are big and I is small."

The supervisor asks her what image she would like to have instead of Calimero, and she mentions with a smile: Pippi Longstocking! Pippi Longstocking is a fictional character in a series of children's books and is adapted into multiple films and television series. She is unconventional, assertive and has superhuman strengths. The supervisee likes the idea of starting to use this metaphor and to become more like Pippi Longstocking. After a while she reports a number of heroics in her role as Pippi and manages to deliver a few reports on time. In addition, she experiences more job satisfaction.

Homework Suggestions

In positive supervision (suggestions for) homework may be given. These are meant to attract the attention of supervisees to focus on those aspects of their experiences and situations that are most useful in finding solutions and reaching their goal. Homework suggestions can, for example, be about reading professional books, self-monitoring of certain undesired and/or desired behavior, doing behavioral tasks, such as the aforementioned *do-as-if task*, or performing certain interventions in working with their clients.

Typically homework suggestions consist of congruent assignments, and as long as the supervisees are motivated to change their behavior this is fine. Stagnation or failure – also in supervision – may be caused when supervisees are not motivated to do certain homework: in that case the supervisor is not adjusting to the motivation to change of the supervisee. As a result problems arise in the alliance: the supervisor – and often also the supervisees – feels irritated, discouraged, or uncertain and start using concepts such as *resistance* and *noncompliance* (see Chapter 8), which soon turns the supervisees into enemies.

In positive supervision only suggestions for homework are given that make sense to the supervisees and are useful to them. The supervisor asks: "Do you think it's a good idea to do something between the sessions?" or "How will you know doing this homework will be useful?" Change usually already takes place during the supervision sessions, therefore doing homework assignments is considered less important in positive supervision than in traditional supervision.

De Shazer (1985, p. 21) states the following about psychotherapy, probably also true about supervision: "We found that we could get as much information when the client did not perform the task as when the client did perform the task. Not only that, we also found that accepting the nonperformance as a message about the client's way of doing things (rather than as a sign of resistance) allowed us to develop a cooperating relationship with clients which might not include task assignments. This was a shock to us because we had assumed that tasks were almost always necessary to achieve behavioral change. Thus, we became more successful with more clients in a fewer number of sessions."

The working relationship between supervisor and supervisees determines the homework suggestions that are given.

- To supervisees in a visitor relationship no homework is given. The supervisor gives compliments for showing up (after all they are involuntary), asks the supervisee what their referrer would like to be different, to what extent they want to comply with that and if they want to come back again.

- To supervisees in a complainant relationship only observational tasks are given: "Observe what you want to keep as it is and does not need to be changed" or "Observe when the problem is nonexistent for a while or is less" or "Notice when little parts of the miracle you described are happening."
- Only to supervisees in a customer relationship are behavioral tasks suggested: "Do more of what works" or "Do something different" or "Do-as-if."

A further explanation of the three types of working relationships is described in Chapter 8. How well supervisees are doing and whether the homework suggestions suit them determines whether the supervisor should continue in the same way or whether something else should be done. Supervisors should always (continue to) adjust their questions and homework tasks in tune with the working relationship they have with their supervisees. In follow-up sessions, it is important to optimize the alliance with their supervisees and maintain and enlarge the progress achieved. Supervisors should check if their homework suggestions were useful and meaningful, and any relapse should be taken care of (see Chapter 7).

Case 26 **Mandated**

There was a case where a manager made it mandatory that a woman receive some supervision. Both agreed that lately the supervisee was not functioning properly, and certainly not when compared to her functioning a year or more ago. Once this mandated supervision began the alliance between the supervisor and the supervisee quickly turned into a customer relationship, in which the supervisee was motivated to change her behavior. In giving feedback she said it had helped her that the supervisor acknowledged the fact that it was her manager who demanded the supervision process in the first place. The supervisor also acknowledged that it was understandable that the supervisee herself was still hesitating whether she really needed this supervision as she was also *mandated* (so at the start there is a visitor relationship).

The supervisor therefore asks not only what the supervisee was prepared to do herself in order to regain her previous level of functioning, but also asks what she thought her manager wanted to see different as a result of the supervision. In this way the manager was, so to speak, also present in the office of the supervisor. By using her own ideas about progress and doing the things she thought her manager wanted her to do, such as an amelioration of the communication with her clients, after some sessions she functioned well again.

In positive supervision two solution-focused assumptions are used: (1) If something works (better), do more of it; and (2) If something doesn't work, do something else. To illustrate this de Shazer (1985, p. 124) gave the example of the policeman who held his breath.

Officers alerted to a prowler at a elementary school Sunday morning found a 10-year old boy wandering around the building. The boy refused to talk, so officers took him in for questioning. When officers were unable to convince him to confess his intent, a mighty battle of wits began between the suspect and the officer. The boy stood firm in the face of the repeated questioning, saying little more than his name. In exasperation, the lieutenant threatened to hold his breath until the boy confessed. This proved to be too much, and the boy blurted out that he had broken into the school to retrieve his homework so he wouldn't get a zero when school opened Monday.

Reporting to Third Parties

Reporting to third parties may consist of supervisees writing letters about their clients to family doctors or to colleagues. Reporting to third parties may also consist of supervisors writing (semi) annual reviews about the supervisees, for example, to the training institutions or to the manager who mandated the supervisees.

In positive supervision supervisees are always involved as much as possible in writing reports, after all, it is about them! Whenever possible, the supervisees write the basic concepts of such letters or reviews first, which may then be supplemented and approved by the supervisor. Supervisees are encouraged to adopt the same attitude towards their clients.

Case 27 Feedback

A supervisee sends me an e-mail stating that her manager wanted me to e-mail my feedback about her back to him/her. I explain to the supervisee and her manager that this is not the way I work as a supervisor, and that I would like to invite the supervisee to formulate the feedback together with me during the next supervision session. I invite the supervisee to make an outline in advance, including the items she thinks are important to her manager and to have already filled out the usual forms as much as possible before we meet.

Supervision via E-mail and/or Skype

Most (peer) supervision consists of sessions where everyone is present. However, supervision may also be carried out when it is not possible for everyone to meet in person, because, for example, the distance between the supervisee and supervisor is too big. In that case, supervision via e-mail (called *e-supervision*) and/or Skype is possible, especially when this is interspersed with some 'live' sessions. Supervisees can easily give their feedback at the end of each session using the Session Rating Scale (SRS, see Chapter 6) by e-mail or Skype. Also the protocols for the first session and follow-up sessions (see Chapter 3 and 7; Appendices 2 and 4) may be applied in supervision via e-mail and/or Skype.

Training of Supervisors

To date there are few specific training courses for supervisors. Most colleagues become a supervisor after a number of years of practical experience, without an additional training course to become a supervisor. There is a discussion going on whether supervisors, like teachers in schools, should take an extra training course or have a special teaching license, or whether their professional competence is sufficient to give good supervision. Often specific competencies are deemed necessary to become a supervisor. Lists of competencies are used as a guideline in the assessment of supervisors by their colleagues or by the educational committees of the associations or institutions they work for.

However, as I described in Chapter 1, from a positive supervision point of view the supervisees should first and foremost determine whether their supervisors are competent, not just their colleagues or the institutions they work for. Therefore these institutions and associations should ask the supervisees for feedback about their supervisors more often than is happening right now. If supervisors underperform in the eyes of their supervisees they should then take mandatory supervision training courses, or their names should be removed from the charter of supervisors of these training institutions and associations.

It goes without saying that all supervisors should continue to develop their skills and should have the desire to become (even) better in their profession, by gaining and applying their knowledge about recent developments. It also goes without saying that the names of supervisors who no longer have the motivation to continue developing their skills should be removed from the charter.

Personal Therapy for Professionals

Besides (peer) supervision many psychotherapy associations make personal therapy for professionals mandatory. This form of therapy focuses on the personal performance of the (candidate) colleague, both in work and in private, and may take place both individually and in groups.

There are different opinions about the usefulness of this kind of therapy. Some find it useful or even necessary; others think it should be eliminated or that at least there should be more transparency about what happens in therapy mandated by a professional association. But this is diametrically opposed to the confidentiality and secrecy in this kind of therapy, and so it seems that the last word about this has not yet been spoken. As an argument in favor of this association-driven therapy professionals become familiar with the role of their clients by being a client themselves. As to the effectiveness of this therapy required by the regulations of a professional association, to date no research has been done.

Positive personal therapy for professionals is different from traditional personal therapy, just as positive supervision is different from traditional supervision. Also here, the focus is on building solutions and enhancing competencies instead of problem-solving and repairing weaknesses. In positive learning therapy the colleagues, as in positive supervision, are seen as coexperts from the start, instead of someone who doesn't know yet and/or cannot perform well yet. Another advantage is that colleagues, by experiencing themselves how positive personal therapy for professionals works, at the same time can start applying this new paradigm in their own work.

Case 28 Perfectionism

In a personal therapy for professionals I ask my colleague what her goal is. She says she wants to be less of a perfectionist at the end of the therapy, to have a better relationship with her mother and to have stopped biting her nails. I invite her to choose whether she wishes to tackle these topics in a problem-focused or solution-focused way. She then chooses to tackle the relationship with her mother and biting her nails in a solution-focused way and her perfectionism in a problem-focused way.

She is the one who determines the order. After a rapid improvement of the relationship with her mother and the nail biting we arrive at the issue of her perfectionism. Because she chooses to tackle this in a problem-focused fashion, I ask her questions about her perfectionism, its possible causes, we make a case-conceptualization and I ask her to monitor how often the (excessive) perfectionism shows. Upon her return, she says she is not very happy with the self-monitoring: the perfectionism is much more frequent than she had estimated. Because it was agreed that she would tackle this issue in a problem-focused way, I invite her to keep on self-monitoring the problem.

> The next session she inquires if it would be OK to deal with her perfectionism in a solution-focused way, to which I consent. She then starts to monitor the exceptions to the problem: when are there moments when she is a little bit less perfectionistic and is able to let go a little bit? Doing this type of self-monitoring cheers her up, and of course these successful moments are found to be present. In addition, the self-monitoring of exceptions to the problem focuses on what already works and may be done again by her in the future.

Personal therapy for professionals usually is a mandatory part of being trained as a therapist and therefore could cause a visitor relationship between the therapist and colleague (see Chapter 8): "I don't have any problems, I honestly wouldn't know what we should discuss, everything is just running smoothly." In that case the task of the therapist is to nevertheless explore with the colleague how the conversation(s) may be most useful to him/her and what (s)he wants to have reached at the end of the therapy to say that it has been worth the effort/time/money (goal formulation, see Chapter 3). If, however, the colleague replies to these questions that (s)he thinks the sessions will not be useful, there is no sense in continuing the therapy and the therapist should terminate the contact.

There may also be a complainant relationship between the therapist and a colleague in personal therapy for professionals. In that case, the colleague wants someone else or something else to change and suffers under the present circumstances, but the colleague is not motivated to change him- or herself. Chapter 8 describes how the therapist may handle this situation.

It has been my experience also that in personal therapy for professionals – both in positive and traditional therapy – it is very effective to ask the colleague to give feedback at the end of every session using the Session Rating Scale (SRS) (see Chapter 6). This is always followed by the question what you as the therapist can do better or different the next session to receive a higher rating.

Summary

- Some practical matters are discussed, such as the supervision agreement, creating an agenda, and writing reports.
- Viewing/listening to video or audio recordings and practical exercises as role-playing, drawing, and making a mind map are explained.
- Information is given about different types of homework suggestions, depending on the working relationship, and how to report to third parties.
- The possibility to supervise via e-mail and/or Skype is discussed.
- From the point of view of positive supervision the assessment and rat-

ing of supervisors should first and foremost be done by their supervisees and not by colleagues, as is now often the case.

- *Positive personal therapy for professionals* is different from traditional
  personal therapy. Also here, the focus is on building solutions instead
  of problem-solving and the colleagues in therapy are considered to be
  coexperts from the start. Also in personal therapy for professionals it
  is effective to ask the colleagues to give feedback at the end of every
  session, using the Session Rating Scale.

Chapter 10
Twenty-Two Frequently Asked Questions

The wise man is not the man who provides the right answers,
but the one who asks the right questions.
Claude Levi-Strauss

Twenty-two frequently asked questions (FAQ) are listed questions along with their answers, all were asked and answered during supervision and training courses.

I don't pretend to have all the right answers and invite you to come up with your own inspiring answers. You are also welcome to e-mail your suggestions to: solutions@fredrikebannink.com

Question 1: What if My Supervisee Has No Goal?

- Ask what you supervisee would like as a result of the supervision.
- Ask what his or her best hopes are and what difference it will make when these hopes are met.
- Ask your supervisee what he or she wants to be different tomorrow, if the miracle question doesn't work.
- Invite your supervisee to ask other people (e.g., colleagues) what his or her goal is according to them.
- Ask about exceptions to the problem (if there is one).
- Invite your supervisee to do more of what works.
- Invite your supervisee to observe what works.
- Ask how your supervisee is coping with the situation.

- Ask your supervisee to exaggerate the problem (if there is one).
- Invite your supervisee to tell you about previous successes in building solutions to see what may be used again in this situation.
- Give your supervisee compliments for showing up and talking to you.
- Ask your supervisee who referred him to you and what he or she thinks the referrer wants to see different as a result of supervision.
- Discuss with your supervisee the disadvantages or possible dangers of change.
- Invite the supervisee to meet with you again in the future.
- Don't give any homework suggestions.
- You may not have a customer relationship with the supervisee. For further suggestions see Chapter 8.

Question 2: What if the Goal of My Supervisee Is Unrealistic?

- If your supervisee has a disability that prevents him or her from reaching the goal then there is not a problem to be solved but a fact of life that has to be dealt with in the best possible way.
- If your supervisee has an unrealistic goal (winning the lotto, wanting someone who died to be alive, wishing the accident had never happened), ask: "Suppose that was a reality, what difference would that make in your life?" Or ask your supervisee what this would mean to him or her.
- Ask yourself whether you are dealing with not just a complaint or wish (to bring about a different feeling or a change in another person) but with an actual goal, the attainment of which lies within the supervisee's control (a positive, concrete, and realistic goal).

Question 3: What if My Supervisee Answers, "I Don't Know"?

- Ask your supervisee: "Suppose you did know, what would you say?"
- Ask your supervisee: "Suppose you did know, what difference will that make?"
- Ask your supervisee: "Suppose I was to ask another person in your life (partner, children, colleagues, best friend), what would they say?"; "Would you be surprised?"; "Which person you know would be least surprised?"; "Who would be most surprised?"
- Agree with your supervisee and say: "Yes, I am asking you some tough questions, please take your time."
- Ask yourself: Is it important for my supervisee to know?

- Ask your supervisee: "How would your life be different if you did know?" or "How would your life be better if you did know?"
- Or say: "Take a guess!"
- Say: "Of course you don't know yet, but what do you think?"
- Tell yourself that something important is probably going on at this point and allow your supervisee more time to come up with an answer.

Question 4: What if My Supervisee Cannot Name Any Personal Strengths?

- Help your supervisee to explore areas of his/her life that are going relatively well, expressing curiosity for all of the supervisee's life, not just problem areas.
- Ask what happens in his/her life that (s)he would like to continue to happen and link that to his/her strengths.
- Then link these areas to supervision goals.
- Ask coping questions and competence questions: How do you manage? How do you cope with this situation? Could the situation be worse? How is it that the situation isn't worse?
- Invite your supervisee to fill out the Values in Action (VIA) Survey of Character Strengths on the Internet (see Chapter 4).
- Use the *third person perspective*: "Suppose you had a twin brother/sister sitting right behind you (or your best friend), what would (s)he say your strengths are?"
- More strategies to invite your supervisee to discover his/her strengths are described in Chapter 4.

Question 5: What if My Supervisee Cannot Find Exceptions to the Problem?

- Do you have a complainant relationship with your supervisee? (see Chapter 8). Then only give observational homework suggestions.
- Ask your supervisee to pay attention to what is going well and should stay the same or pay attention to what goes on in his/her life that (s)he would like to continue to happen.
- Ask your supervisee to observe the positive moments in his/her life or work so that (s)he can talk about them next time you meet.
- Ask your supervisee to pay attention to the times when things are going (a little bit) better so that (s)he can talk about them next time.

- See if the goal is formulated in positive, concrete, and realistic terms.
- Ask scaling questions: "Observe when you are one point higher on the scale and what you and/or (significant) others are doing differently then."
- Ask your supervisee to pay attention to what gives him/her hope that the problem can be solved;
- Use prediction homework: "Predict what tomorrow will be like, find an explanation for why the day turned out the way it did tomorrow evening, and then make a new prediction for the following day." If the prediction was correct: "How did you know?" If the prediction was not correct: "What was it that made the day different from what you predicted?"
- With a supervisee in a complainant relationship, who thinks the other person is the problem and needs to change: Pay attention to the times when the other person does more of what you want, to what is different then, and to what (s)he sees you do then that is helpful to him/her.
- Ask your supervisee to pay attention to what the other person does that is useful or pleasant and to the difference it makes, so that this can be discussed the next time you meet.
- Have your supervisee ask other people around him/her what exceptions they see.
- Ask your supervisee: "Suppose you could find an exception, what difference will that make?"
- See Appendix 3 for a protocol for finding exceptions pertaining to the goal and/or pertaining to the problem.

Question 6: What if My Supervisee Has Not Done His/Her Homework?

- The importance of homework as seen in, for example, traditional supervision models is no longer deemed useful (see Chapter 9).
- Ask yourself if homework suggestions will generate more information than if the supervisee doesn't perform homework.
- Accept nonperformance as a message about your supervisee's way of doing things rather than as a sign of resistance.
- Say to your supervisee that you are sure (s)he must have a good reason for not doing his/her homework and invite him/her to tell you more about this reason.
- Remember to keep a positive alliance with your supervisee, even without him/her doing any homework.
- Only provide feedback for the supervisee to reflect on, or assign an observational homework task. Your supervisee may not yet or may no longer be in a customer relationship with you (see Chapter 8).

- Do you want too much too soon? Look for smaller changes, use scaling questions regarding the goal or the exceptions, or counsel the supervisee not to move too fast.

Question 7: What if My Supervisee Says, "You Tell me What to Do, You Are the Supervisor!"

- Ask your supervisee if in the past it has been useful when other people told him/her what to do.
- Ask your supervisee if, before you offer some suggestions, (s)he is willing to answer a few questions.
- Then ask him/her about exceptions to the problem, his/her competencies, and successes in the past.
- Keep your supervisee in the role of the coexpert. For example, explain that others have solved similar problems as the supervisee has through x, y, or z. Invite your supervisee to reflect on which solution (s)he may find most useful.
- Invite your supervisee to do some behavioral experiments and to observe what difference they make. For example, ask your supervisee to *pretend the miracle has happened* (if the miracle questions is asked, see Chapter 3, or if the supervisee would be higher on the scale, see Chapter 5 and 9).
- Take a cautious stance: "I think I have an idea, but I am sure you have already tried it and it probably didn't help much…did you ever try to…?"

Question 8: What if My Supervisee Comes Up With a Hypothesis or Wants to Find an Explanation for What Is Wrong With Him/Her or With the Client?

- De Shazer, cofounder of SFBT, states that when you feel a hypothesis coming up, you should take two aspirins, go to bed and hope it will be over tomorrow.
- Normalize: remember we human beings are explanation-seekers.
- Also keep in mind that you do not need to find an explanation in order to be able to help yourself or your client reach his/her goal.
- Instead ask your supervisee/client: "Suppose you were to have an explanation, what difference would that make?"
- Ask: "How would an explanation be helpful to you?"
- Ask: "What part of the explanation do you already have?"

- Ask your supervisee what (s)he can do to come up with information that may be useful in finding the explanation (s)he wants.
- Ask what explanations others have given and if or how that has been helpful.
- Ask how you as his/her supervisor might be helpful in helping him/her to come up with an explanation.
- The focus on explanations may indicate that there is a complainant relationship with this supervisee (see Chapter 8).

Question 9: What if My Supervisee Returns to Problem-Talk all the Time?

- Don't get discouraged, because this happens quite often as many supervisees still think this is the aim of supervision.
- Explain to your supervisee that there is a new vision about supervision: not just the problem-focused vision, in which the focus is on what doesn't work and deficits and how to repair those, but also the positive vision, in which the focus is on what works, strengths, and how to build on those.
- Keep in mind that you as a supervisor don't need to know much about the problems of your supervisee when working from a positive supervision point of view.
- Gently interrupt your supervisee and say: "OK, we'll come back to that." Once your supervisee has moved on to a more clearly defined goal or can find exceptions to the problem, often there is no need or wish any more to return to the topic.
- Ask you supervisee how long/how many sessions (s)he thinks necessary, before (s)he can move on from talking about his/her problem to starting to talk about what (s)he wants and his/her preferred future.
- Consider whether you have a customer relationship with your supervisee or maybe a complainant relationship and if so, adjust your interventions accordingly (see Chapter 8);
- Ask your supervisee: "How do you think that talking about your problem will help you reach your goal?"
- See if the goal is formulated in positive, concrete, and realistic terms.
- Say to your supervisee that (s)he must have a good reason to keep talking about the problem and invite him/her to tell you about this reason.
- Ask: "Suppose you said everything you want to say about your problem, what would be changed/what would be better for you?"

Question 10: What if the Supervision Stagnates?

- If your approach doesn't work, stop and do something else. Continuing with an approach that is not working and doing more of the same when there is no progress are some of the pathways to impossibility, as described in Chapter 5.
- Remember that Einstein stated: "Insanity is doing the same thing over and over again, expecting different results."
- If you don't have a customer relationship with your supervisee, ask yourself if you as a supervisor are motivated to change your behavior, in order to ameliorate the working relationship. If not, refer your supervisee to a colleague, because your supervision will not be helpful for your supervisee.
- Remember that psychotherapists are very bad at identifying deteriorating clients and routinely overestimate their own effectiveness. The same might be true for supervisors.
- Don't assume that deterioration of your supervisee's situation comes before the situation gets better. Instead, research shows this is an indicator that portends a final negative outcome.
- Ask your supervisee the questions for stagnation and failure in Chapter 5.
- Invite others into the conversation (partner, children, friends);
- Ask your supervisee to give you feedback at the end of every session (see Chapter 6).

Question 11: What if I Become Irritated, Discouraged, or Feel Uncertain?

- If you feel irritated, discouraged, or uncertain (*countertransference*) you need to focus more on the alliance with your supervisee.
- Ask yourself what *you* can do differently to enhance the alliance (see Chapter 8), instead of thinking what the supervisee should do differently.
- Ask your supervisee what you could do differently to enhance the alliance.
- Ask yourself: "Suppose I would be one point higher on the scale of the alliance than I am now, what will I do differently then? How will my supervisee react differently? And how will I react differently to that?"
- Give your supervisee more compliments by focusing on his/her strengths, successes, and competences.
- Look for exceptions and previous successes in your alliance with the supervisee.
- Ask a supervisor or colleagues in peer supervision what you can do differently to enhance the alliance.

- Ask your supervisee to give you feedback at the end of every session (see Chapter 6).

Question 12: What if My Supervisee Has Very Complex Problems?

- Remember that complex problems don't need complex solutions and that you as a supervisor don't need to know as much as possible about your supervisee's problems in order to effectively help him/her.
- Follow Einstein's constraint: "Everything should be kept as simple as possible, but no simpler."
- Acknowledge the suffering caused by the problems.
- Ask questions about his/her goal, exceptions, scaling, competences etc, to invite your supervisee to talk about what (s)he want to see different in the future.
- Find out what type of working alliance you have with your supervisee and adjust your interventions and homework suggestions (if any) to that.
- Refer your supervisee to a psychotherapist if necessary.

Question 13: What if My supervisee Does Not Want to Talk About What Is Bothering Him/Her or What If There Is a Secret?

- Put your supervisee at ease and respect that (s)he is not (yet) ready (and perhaps will never be ready) to tell you what is bothering him/her.
- Don't think it is necessary for your supervisee to unveil his/her secret to you.
- Ask your supervisee: "Suppose you do tell me what is bothering you, what difference would that make?"
- Ask your supervisee: "Suppose there is a solution, how would your life/work be different?"

Question 14: Does Positive Supervision Pay Any Attention to the Past?

- Yes, positive supervision does pay attention to the past: not to find the causes of problems, but to find previous successes and competencies.

- Keep in mind that a past–present–future timeline is too simplistic and that the present is also shaped by the future (e.g., positive or negative *self-fulfilling prophecies*).
- Keep in mind that the past is only the memory of previous experiences and that the future is only the expectation of experiences to come while in the present. We only have access to the present.
- Positive supervision can change the meaning of what happened in the past. To make that happen it is not always necessary to talk about the (traumatic) past. When the present ameliorates and your supervisee becomes more confident in the future, the (traumatic) past becomes less poisonous.
- Ask for example: "How will you know that what happened is no longer holding you back in your life?" or "How will you know that you are doing justice to yourself and your possibilities, despite what was done to you?"
- Keep your supervisee in the expert position by asking, for example: "How did you succeed to make changes before?"; "Which personal strengths did you use?"; "When else in the past have you seen yourself drawing on those qualities in a way that is useful to you?"; "Having made these changes, looking back to the time before the change, what tells you that you always did have the capacity to make these changes?"
- Ask questions from the *third person perspective*: "Of all those who have known you in your past, who would be least surprised by the changes that you have made?"; "What is it that those people knew that others perhaps did not know about you and your possibilities?"; "And who would be the most surprised?"
- Ask the *miracle question* and invite your supervisee to describe the miracle (10 on the scale): "What will you remember, looking back, that tells you that you always knew you could do this?"

Question 15: Can Positive Supervision Be Integrated With Problem-Focused Supervision?

- The answer to this question depends on what is meant by integrating. The answer is negative if it means that the positive vision can be fitted into the problem-focused vision. The answer is positive if it means that the positive vision can be combined with the problem-focused one (as an example of this see Appendix 8).
- Keep in mind that you as a supervisor always have the choice to talk about problems (*problem-talk*) or to talk about strengths and solutions (*solutions-talk*).

- Keep in mind that acknowledging the problem is important, because your supervisee will feel heard and understood and that this is different from exploring the problem.
- *Positive diagnosis* is different from the diagnosis of problems: diagnosis is about goal analysis instead of problem analysis; about strengths instead of weaknesses; about functional behavior analysis of exceptions to the problem instead of the problem itself; about signals defining progress instead of signals defining stagnation or relapse; and about the working relationship with the supervisee (Bannink, 2013, 2012).
- Keep in mind that positive supervision transcends diagnostics and that you as a supervisor are an expert in asking useful questions.

Question 16: How Do I Cooperate With Problem-Focused Colleagues?

- Remember it is very likely that many of your colleagues are still thinking and acting in a problem-focused way. Therefore, they place greater emphasis on problems (and are more prone to finding problems).
- Keep in mind that it is not useful to fight the often deeply rooted vision of your colleagues. Instead, there should be studies of outcomes to show which vision prevails.
- Make sure you keep your supervisee's goals in mind and that this goal is always your guide. Meetings with your colleagues may get bogged down in a lengthy discussion of problems or complaints about another person or other people.
- Establish a positive framework. Making the (hidden) positive motivation of everyone involved explicit may put your colleagues at ease and allow them to work in a goal-oriented manner.
- Compliment your colleagues and always explicitly express your appreciation of the progress being made and their collaboration.
- Regularly point out the successes and strengths of your colleagues and summarize them. Be generous.
- Use positive *guerrilla actions*. Now and then show your colleagues without explaining too much, what it is exactly that you do when using positive supervision. For example, show them that you ask about exceptions to the problem and that you highlight areas of strengths and resources of your supervisees.
- Remember to be the change you want to see in your team/organization.

Question 17: Do Supervisors Never Give Advice in Positive Supervision?

- Positive supervision is not *problem phobic*. Of course in positive supervision advice may be given, only the timing if different from traditional supervision (see Chapter 2).
- Ask your supervisee how they learn best. If this includes giving some advice now and then, this is the best way to connect to what is important for your supervisee.
- Invite your supervisee to first explore and use his/her own expertise, even if (s)he invites you to use yours as a supervisor (also see Question 7). For example, ask about exceptions or moments when the alliance with his/her client was better. Indeed, the supervisee is regarded as a coexpert from the start of supervision.
- In positive supervision the supervisor only gives advice when invited by the supervisee to do so (see Chapter 2).

Question 18: Are Problems Never Discussed in Positive Supervision?

- Again: positive supervision is not *problem phobic*. Problematic issues (the supervisees' own problems or problems with their clients) may be put forward. The supervisor listens respectfully and acknowledges the fact that this problem causes them to suffer: "I understand this must be difficult for you. How do you cope?"
- The supervisor, however, actively listens to openings in the problem story. As soon as possible the supervisor asks what the supervisee wants to have instead of the problem. The supervisor does not ask for details of the problem (of the supervisees or their clients).
- Often supervisees think that it is necessary to tell in detail what is wrong with themselves or their clients and that the supervisor will provide suggestions or advice about the diagnosis and/or approach, as is common in traditional problem-focused supervision.
- Sometimes supervisees have to get used to the idea that they are asked about their own ideas about what works. Supervisors should not think too quickly that supervisees have no clue or do not possess the necessary competence.
- Ask your supervisees how they learn best: by receiving advice, by thinking about what might work themselves, by experimenting. Adjust the supervision to what works best for them.

- Positive supervision is not about solving any problems the supervisee has with clients, it is about how supervisees can optimize their functioning in working with their clients.
- Use solutions-talk instead of problem-talk as much as possible.

Question 19: Is There a Risk That the Supervisee Will Find the Supervisor Implausible or Annoying When Using Positive Supervision?

- Positive supervision is not about looking at the world through rose-colored glasses: there is also room for criticism and advice.
- In Chapter 2 the *positivity ratio* was described, stating there is a ceiling to positivity: 11:1. However, this ceiling was found in the USA, in other countries this ceiling may be lower.
- Research shows that in all kinds of social situations – I assume supervision included – the golden rule applies: 5:1 is the most effective, in other words five compliments, affirmations, etc. against one disapproval, criticism, or negative remark (see Chapter 2).

Question 20: Are the Perceptions of Supervisees Emphasized Too Much in Positive Supervision?

- Just as in SFBT the perception of clients is more important than the perception of their therapists, in positive supervision the perception of supervisees is more important than the perception of the supervisor (see Chapter 2).
- This perspective can be found in the questionnaire for supervisors (see Chapter 1 and Appendix 7).
- Supervisees, instead of their colleagues and institutions, should first and foremost do the appreciation of supervisors.
- Right from the start of the positive supervision the supervisees are seen as coexperts and not just at the end of supervision, as is the case in other models.
- If you as a supervisor want to be the only expert in the room, making analyses, hypotheses, and interpretations of problems of your supervisees' clients, and then give advice on how your supervisees should solve these problems, a problem-focused supervision model probably suits you better.

Question 21: Is Enough Attention Paid in Positive Supervision to the Relationship Between the Problem and the Solution?

- Einstein already stated that you cannot solve a problem with the same kind of thinking that created it.
- The problem-solving *cause-and-effect model* is very straightforward and useful when things are simply related, stable, and mechanical, but not so useful when things are complex, interactive, and continuously changing.
- Sometimes there is no (necessary) connection between the problem and the solution or sometimes we may identify the cause but cannot remove it.
- Some authors don't even use the term *solution*, because this suggests there is a problem (de Bono, 1985; Walter & Peller, 2000). They rather speak of *possibilities* and *preferences*.
- In *designing a positive outcome* (the goal: the preferred future) the cause-and-effect model is no longer used. One looks forward to what may be created instead of looking back at what is already there (and needs to be repaired).

Question 22: What if My Supervisee Does Something That Is Dangerous, Harmful, or Unethical?

- In each model of supervision it should be clear who is responsible. This should already be stated in the supervision contract.
- Supervisors should become more directive than usual in positive supervision in situations where supervisees show dangerous, harmful, or unethical behavior.
- Take your time to discuss this behavior with your supervisee in an open dialog and explain what you think (s)he should do differently.
- Always behave in accordance with your conscience and your estimation of the situation.
- Keep in mind that it is only on the rarest occasions that taking away the self-determination of your supervisee is necessary.

Chapter 11
Supervisees Speak Out

Tell me and I will forget;
Show me and I may remember;
Involve me and I will understand.
Confucius

In this chapter five Dutch supervisees speak out (this book was published in Dutch in 2012). All are psychologists and have been taking part in positive supervision in the context of the training to become a psychotherapist for the Dutch Association for Behavioural and Cognitive Therapies (VGCt). Some of the supervisees make a comparison with the problem-focused supervision they experienced earlier. Excerpts from their reports can be found in the previous chapters of this book. I am thankful for their willingness to accept my invitation to describe their experiences with positive supervision and for their permission to use their observations in this book.

"Turning limitations into possibilities, thinking in challenges instead of problems, focusing on solutions instead of stagnation. ... isn't it a bit forced? Isn't this way of looking at things just for some trippy types, not for more sober people like me? These are just a few of the prejudices I had to overcome when several years ago I started attending a training course about solution focused brief therapy as part of my training to become a cognitive behavioral therapist. These prejudices quickly disappeared when during this day Fredrike Bannink invited us to experience the differences between the problem-focused and solution-focused approach.

For me this meant a valuable addition because I am pretty good at unraveling problems. What is more delicious and satisfying than filleting a complex problem? By doing that I sometimes forget to look for moments when the problem didn't happen or what small steps have been taken in the desired direction.

Not long afterwards I was given the opportunity to experience how positive supervision works. And how well it works! This supervision not only offered me a very nice addition in working with my clients, but also helped me in my own development as a psychotherapist. First and foremost it was helpful in formulating a clear goal: what is it I wanted to achieve? In addition it was helpful by not only shedding light on competencies I don't (yet) possess, but also by especially highlighting competencies which show that the desired development is already under way as well as revealing which competencies I want to strengthen further. For example, I became more aware of the influence language has on my clients.

I am pleased that positive supervision complemented my heavy problem-focused approach. The result is that I now have a multicolor palette of approaches available to me. And if nowadays I want to unravel problems again, I focus much more often on analyzing situations when the problem doesn't exist. I noticed that this is a pleasant way of working for my clients. I do hope that other supervisees will experience the same as I did through this book."

Petra Joosse

"My supervisor taught me the power of an optimistic, realistic, and hopeful approach. Positive supervision invited me to reflect on what I wanted to achieve and how I can rely on my own competencies and strengths. I was encouraged to explore what I had already achieved in working with my clients, what works, what I want to continue doing, and what I would like to do differently. If I compare this approach of supervision with the more traditional problem-focused supervision for me the difference lies mainly in two points: the motivational effect the focus on positive cognitions and behavior has and the confidence in my own power to devise appropriate solutions. Changing the focus from an analysis of problem behavior to an analysis of positive and successful behavior and cognitions reinforces my positive emotions. It strengthens my hope of a positive outcome and my confidence that this is feasible using small steps forward. The acknowledgement of how difficult some situations are helps me to continue with a complex case, strengthens the idea that I am on the right track, and helps me getting new bright ideas. I am often surprised by the simplicity of the solutions. It often turns out to be easy to generate and implement new ideas and interventions. In problem-focused supervision I learned from the 'sharp minds' of my supervisors; in positive supervision I learned to use my own 'sharp mind.' This helps me to become more independent and more effective in creating and supporting change. At the same time, I experienced what effort it takes to do things this way and how helpful my supervisor was in this process by appreciating me and giving me lots of positive reinforcement.

The supervision was an example for me in how I wanted to work and helped me to always respectfully look for opportunities and possibilities in my work with families, to highlight and appreciate the smallest positive changes, even if there is sometimes a big tangle of problems.

By looking with families at exceptions to the problem, moments when they do well, and having confidence in their own capacities and resources, it is possible to slowly work towards often unexpected major changes."

Silke Fromm

"How fragile and uncertain I was, when I got a job as an intern at a mental health institution. I just started my training as a cognitive behavioral therapist and had only a little experience. I saw the job as a great opportunity to gain experience. Every week a meeting was held about the new and ongoing treatments and once every couple of weeks I received supervision. The team worked in a problem-focused way: their focus was on the clients' problems and on diagnosis. The diagnosis was stated to the client right after the intake; there was almost no room for the wishes of the clients about their treatment. Supervision sessions were in accordance with the problem-focused view: the supervisor looked at the errors and mistakes I made and at capacities, which I didn't have (yet). When my imperfections were highlighted I always had the urge to start defending myself. This, however, was like fighting a losing battle: a mistake was a mistake and 'I should have known better.' Every time I noticed that I cringed and I started even to feel anxious about the supervision sessions. Despite the fact that my clients appreciated my treatments, I grew more and more uncertain. The last months of my internship I went to my work and supervision with abdominal pain.

How different was my experience when I met a supervisor for the first time who worked from the solution-focused and positive psychology point of view. I remember well how different the atmosphere was and the attitude of the supervisor in relation to me, the supervisee. I was asked about my goals for the supervision. Soon came up my perfectionism and fear of rejection. By using a scale of 10–0, we examined how far I already was in completing my goals. I was asked how I was able to give a 6 on the scale instead of a 1 or 0. We examined what competencies I owned and in what situations I managed to act according to my goals.

I was surprised: we did not look at my 'weaknesses,' but rather at my skills. I suddenly felt a lot more capable in my work than I previously thought I was. I even became even more surprised when the supervisor explained to me what the purpose of supervision is: that you feel competent in your profession and are able work independently as a psychotherapist.

Speaking from a purely physical point-of-view, solution-focused and problem-focused supervision have a totally different effect. When your imperfections are highlighted the focus is on the negative. It's like a parent – the supervisor is hierarchically superior to the supervisee – who is correcting you.

You become small again and instead of an upright position you shrink a little, making breathing more difficult.

Your self-efficacy is affected and the self-doubt that was already there enlarges. This affects your functioning at work and might even be noticed by your clients. Clients may get the idea that you are not sure how you can help them solve their problems.

However, when your competencies are highlighted, you become a bit bigger; you grow, breathing becomes easier, your self-efficacy increases, and the issues you first were not sure about become smaller and less problematic. This also has an effect on your work; you have the courage to apply new techniques and make the impression to your clients you are confident and skilled in helping to solve their problems. And this is precisely the purpose of the supervision.

In positive supervision several things make you grow as a supervisee and feel more competent. Because of the positive focus the atmosphere in supervision is more relaxed. Your qualities are positively reinforced and successes are highlighted. You leave the supervision with a positive feeling and a stronger self-efficacy. Anxiety and uncertainty change into enthusiasm and confidence, which ensures you reach the desired future earlier, which is to be a competent professional. The strict hierarchy with its focus on errors disappears; there is a more equal relationship, in which you both bandy thoughts around about certain issues and possible solutions. Because there is also room for the person of the supervisee you feel recognized and respected. Personal circumstances or characteristics that complicate working with clients are addressed, so that you feel free to work properly.

Assuming that you are learning a profession where your passion lies, supervision is also a place to share enthusiasm for the profession. In this way supervision becomes a fun part of the training, and experiencing a shared passion creates more meaning in your work. I literally felt the urge to run to the supervision sessions to share with my supervisor new developments and my growth. After enthusiastically sharing an applied technique she once remarked: 'Who do you think was more surprised that it worked out so well, you or your client?'

In this way supervision becomes a positive learning experience, where you are stimulated to want to learn even more and get better at what you are doing. The uncertainty and self-doubt that I experienced at the start of the supervision disappeared and changed into self-efficacy.

You grow into a professional who has confidence in herself and the way she functions. In other words, you became competent to work independently and to complete the training feeling satisfied."

Fleur van der Goes

"From the start I came into contact with the power of working in a solution-focused way, because my first supervision session began in this vein. During a training course of cognitive behavioral therapy I was introduced to solution-focused brief therapy, and I feel strong when I think of my answer to the miracle question, when I describe exceptions to the problem, when I reflect on where I am on the scale from 10–0 and which steps I can take to move me to a higher point on the scale. I feel competent and the urge to do more of it is great. Suddenly I realized I had more competencies as a therapist than I previously thought I had. By experiencing what positive supervision does to you, I became instantly excited to also use this approach in the treatments with my clients.

During supervision I realized that little words could make a difference. My supervisor pays a lot of attention to the right wording. In the beginning this felt a bit unpleasant, because she often corrected me (with a smile). When I watched my language closely during my treatments I noticed that this had a positive effect on the treatment and the state of mind of my clients. This ensured that later on I was actually happy about being corrected by my supervisor.

In supervision we often talked about the effect of the use of the Session Rating Scale. By filling out the SRS myself, I really experienced what exactly this effect is. At the start it is strange when a supervisor asks you to provide feedback on the supervision. Also the question 'What can I do differently or better next time to get a higher point on the scale?' was unfamiliar. The first time I didn't dare to say what that might be. The next time, however, I did give feedback and it turned out to be very nice. By doing so we worked more focused on my goals and I got more out of the supervision. It also gives me a good feeling that the supervisor asks me what I want and how I want it. This influences our working relationship in a positive way.

I find it very valuable that positive supervision places so much emphasis on the working relationship. During supervision you learn to pay close attention to the alliance with your clients from the start. In previous supervisions I was not used to paying attention to the working relationship as having a major influence on deciding which steps you take or don't take in psychotherapy. By consciously paying attention I learned to take different steps when a client doesn't cooperate or when there is stagnation. Earlier on I would have done more of what isn't working by continuing to apply a protocol.

Positive supervision gives me strength and pleasure. I am always amazed by the myriad of solution-focused questions and the positive approach. This supervision gives me a sense of empowerment."

Sanne van Beek

"My previous supervisor worked in a problem-focused way and sometimes mixed this approach with a few solution-focused questions and elements.

When I said goodbye to this supervisor after more than a year and started positive supervision, I did not quite know what to expect.

From the first minute it was clear that this supervision was going to be very different. Instead of discussing a therapy by naming the problem of the client, making a holistic theory and problem-focused functional behavior analysis, in each therapy I wanted to discuss I got the question: 'What is the goal of this therapy?'; 'What does this client want to achieve, what should it bring him or her?' This sounds very straightforward, yet I noticed that this question is not always asked explicitly in my therapies. Therefore my clients and I sometimes had different goals in mind. I work with youth who can no longer live at home; they often have a long history of being helped by professionals. For these youth especially it is very important to have the idea that psychotherapy helps them to achieve their goals. Within positive supervision this is always one of the major points of attention. Not just the working relationship with the clients, but also the working relationship with the environment of these youngsters is an important topic in the supervision. You may have a customer relationship with a youngster, but this may not be the case with the group leaders of the institutions these youngsters live in. By first focusing in positive supervision and then in psychotherapies on these topics, I notice that my clients are more motivated. They work on their own goals and the best part is that they themselves come up with great ideas of how they want to achieve those goals and what they need to do to get there.

My experience is that many clients complete their therapies with a positive experience. My own experiences and my role during therapy are of course also focused on in supervision. The question: 'What is your role in the success of your client, what did you do to make this therapy successful?' helps me to understand my therapeutic skills, to enhance my self-efficacy as a therapist and to be enthusiastic in the work I am doing."

Hanneke Krul

Chapter 12
Epilogue

A Zen student came to a wide river.

When he saw his Master on the other side, he called:

"Master, how do I get to the other side?"

"Don't bother," said the Master, "You're already on the other side."

The road to positive supervision begins with taking the first small step. Aristotle has already suggested that it is possible to excel by repeating small positive steps over and over again. Which small positive steps have you already taken? Which part of the road have you already traveled and how did you like it? How can you build from there? Which part of the road do you want travel further? To investigate this you may ask yourself the following questions, in which the perspective of your supervisees is key:

- What will my supervisees say I do that works? What else?
- What do I think I do that works? What else?
- What will my supervisees tell me I should keep doing and shouldn't change?
- What do I want to keep doing? What do I not want to change?
- Where will my supervisees say I am on a scale of 10–0, where 10 means doing positive supervision and 0 means doing traditional problem-focused supervision?
- Where do I put myself on the same scale?
- What will my supervisees say about how I was able to get to that point on the scale?
- What are my ideas about how I was able to reach that point on the scale?
- Where on the scale do my supervisees want me to be in the future?
- Where on the scale do I want to be in the future?
- What will my supervisees say I will be doing differently or better when I am one point higher on the scale?

- Suppose I am one point higher on the scale, what do I think I will do differently or better?
- What will my supervisees say I should do to reach one point higher on the scale?
- What do I think I should do to reach one point higher on the scale?
- What and who can help me to get to a higher point on the scale?

This book aims to make supervision better, more meaningful, and more fun. When you as a supervisor, a facilitator or a participant in peer supervision apply the steps of positive supervision and repeat them over and over again, you will notice that it is possible to excel in your profession.

You may already be on the other side of the river!

References

Allen, R. E., & Allen, S. D. (1997). *Winnie-the-Pooh on Success*. New York, NY: Dutton.

Anderson, S. A., Schlossberg, M., & Rigazio-DiGilio, S. (2000). Family therapy trainees' evaluations of their best and worst supervision experiences. *Journal of Marital and Family Therapy, 26*(1), 79–91. http://doi.org/10.1111/j.1752-0606.2000.tb00278.x

Aristotle (1998). *Nicomachean Ethics*. Mineola, NY: Dover Publications.

Arts, W., Hoogduin, C. A. L., Keijsers, G. P. J., Severeijnen, R., & Schaap, C. (1994). A quasi-experimental study into the effect of enhancing the quality of the patient-therapist relationship in the outpatient treatment of obsessive-compulsive neurosis. In S. Brogo & L. Sibilia (Eds.), *The patient-therapist relationship: Its many dimensions*. Roma, Italy: Consiglio Nazionale delle Ricerche.

Bakker, J. M., Bannink, F. P., & Macdonald, A. (2010). Solution-focused psychiatry. *The Psychiatrist, 34*, 297–300. http://doi.org/10.1192/pb.bp.109.025957

Bandura, A., Ross, D., & Ross, S. A. (1961). Transmission of aggression through imitation of aggressive models. *Journal of Abnormal and Social Psychology, 63*, 575–582. http://doi.org/10.1037/h0045925

Bannink, F. P. (2006). *Oplossingsgerichte mediation* [Solution-focused mediation]. Amsterdam, The Netherlands: Pearson.

Bannink, F. P. (2007a). *Gelukkig zijn en geluk hebben. Zelf oplossingsgericht werken*. [Being happy and being lucky: Solution-focused self-help]. Amsterdam, The Netherlands: Pearson.

Bannink, F. P. (2007b). Solution-focused brief therapy. *Journal of Contemporary Psychotherapy, 37*(2), 87–94. http://doi.org/10.1007/s10879-006-9040-y

Bannink, F. P. (2008a). Posttraumatic success: Solution-focused brief therapy. *Brief Treatment and Crisis Intervention, 7*, 1–11.

Bannink, F. P. (2008b). Solution-focused mediation: The future with a difference. *Conflict Resolution Quarterly, 25*(2), 163–183. http://doi.org/10.1002/crq.203

Bannink, F. P. (2009a). *Positieve psychologie in de praktijk* [Positive psychology in practice]. Amsterdam, The Netherlands: Hogrefe Uitgevers.

Bannink, F. P. (2009b). *Praxis der Lösungs-fokussierten Mediation* [Praxis of solution-focused mediation]. Stuttgart, Germany: Concadora Verlag.

Bannink, F. P. (2010a). *Oplossingsgericht leidinggeven* [Solution-focused leadership]. Amsterdam, The Netherlands: Pearson.

Bannink, F. P. (2010b). *1001 Solution-focused questions: Handbook for solution-focused interviewing*. New York, NY: Norton.

Bannink, F. P. (2010c). *Handbook of solution focused conflict management*. Cambridge, MA: Hogrefe Publishing.

Bannink, F. P. (2012a). *Praxis der Positiven Psychologie* [Praxis of Positive Psychology]. Göttingen, Germany: Hogrefe.

Bannink, F. P. (2012b). *Practicing positive CBT. From reducing distress to building success*. Oxford, UK: Wiley. http://doi.org/10.1002/9781118328941

Bannink, F. P. (2012c). *Positieve supervisie en intervisie* [Positive supervision and peer supervision]. Amsterdam, The Netherlands: Hogrefe Uitgevers.

Bannink, F. P. (2013). *Oplossingsgerichte vragen. Handboek oplossingsgerichte gespreksvoering* (3rd Rev. ed.) [Solution-focused Questions. Handbook for solution-focused interviewing]. Amsterdam, The Netherlands: Pearson.

Bannink, F. P. (2014a). Positive CBT: From reducing distress to building success. *Journal of Contemporary Psychotherapy, 44*, 1–8. http://doi.org/10.1007/s10879-013-9239-7

Bannink, F. P. (2014b). *Post traumatic success: Positive psychology and solution focused strategies to help clients survive and thrive.* New York, NY: Norton.

Bannink, F. P., & Jackson, P. Z. (2011). Positive psychology and solution focus – Looking at similarities and differences. Interaction. *The Journal of Solution Focus in Organisations, 3*(1), 8–20.

Bannink, F. P., & McCarthy, J. (2014, May 16). The solution-focused taxi. *Counseling Today.* Retrieved from http://ct.counseling.org/2014/05/the-solution-focused-taxi/

Barrell, J. J., & Ryback, D. (2008). *Psychology of champions.* Westport, CT: Praeger.

Beck, A. T., Weissman, A., Lester, D., & Trexles, L. (1974). The measurement of pessimism: The Hopelessness Scale. *Journal of Consulting and Clinical Psychology, 42,* 861–865. http://doi.org/10.1037/h0037562

Bellini, S., & Akullian, J. (2007). A meta-analysis of video modeling and video self-modeling interventions for children and adolescents with autism spectrum disorders. *Exceptional Children, 73*(3), 264–287. http://doi.org/10.1177/001440290707300301

Berg, I. K., & Steiner, T. (2003). *Children's solutions work.* New York, NY: Norton.

Bernard, J. M., & Goodyear, R. K. (2009). *Fundamentals of clinical supervision.* Boston, MA: Allyn & Bacon.

Beunderman, R., & Maas, F. van der (Eds.). (2011) *Supervisie in de GGZ* [Supervision in mental health care]. Assen, The Netherlands: Van Gorcum.

Beutler, L. E., Malik, M. L., Alimohamed, S., Harwood, T. M., Talebi, H., & Noble, S. (2004). Therapist variables. In M. J. Lambert (Ed.), *Bergin and Garfield's handbook of psychotherapy and behavior change* (pp. 227–306). New York, NY: Wiley.

Bono, E. de (1985). *Conflicts: A better way to resolve them.* London, UK: Penguin.

Bordin, E. S. (1979). The generalizability of the psychodynamic concept of the working alliance. *Psychotherapy: Theory, Research and Practice, 16,* 252–260. http://doi.org/10.1037/h0085885

Chartier, E. (1938). Propos sur la Religion, no 74.

Clement, P. W. (1994). Quantative evaluation of 26 years of private practice. *Professional Psychology: Research and Practice, 25*(2), 173–176. http://doi.org/10.1037/0735-7028.25.2.173

Csikszentmihalyi, M. (1990). *Flow: The psychology of optimal experience.* New York, NY: Harper & Row.

Dam, L. van (2010). *Oplossingsgerichte intervisie* [Solution-focused peer supervision]. Amsterdam, The Netherlands: Nelissen.

De Jong, P., & Berg, I. K. (2002). *Interviewing for solutions.* Belmont, CA: Thomson.

Den Haan, R., & Bannink, F. P. (2012). *Handboek oplossingsgerichte gespreksvoering met ouderen* [Handbook solution-focused interviewing with elderly clients]. Amsterdam, The Netherlands: Pearson.

de Shazer, S. (1984). The death of resistance. *Family Process, 23,* 79–93.

de Shazer, S. (1985). *Keys to solution in brief therapy.* New York, NY: Norton.

de Shazer, S. (1988). *Clues: Investigating solutions in brief therapy.* New York, NY: Norton.

de Shazer, S. (1991). *Putting difference to work.* New York, NY: Norton.

de Shazer, S. (1994). *Words were originally magic.* New York, NY: Norton.

Dijksterhuis, A. (2007). *Het slimme onbewuste* [The smart unconscious]. Amsterdam, The Netherlands: Bert Bakker.

Duncan, B. L. (2005). *What's right with you: Debunking dysfunction and changing your life.* Derfield Beach, FL: Health Communication.

Duncan, B. L., Miller, S. D., & Sparks, A. (2004). *The heroic client: A revolutionary way to improve effectiveness through client-directed, outcome-informed therapy.* New York, NY: Jossey-Bass.

Dweck, C. (2006). *Mindset: The new psychology of success.* New York, NY: Random House.

Flora, S. R. (2000). Praise's magic reinforcement ratio: Five to one gets the job done. *The Behaviour Analyst Today, 1*, 64–69.

Frank, J. D. (1974). Psychotherapy: The restoration of morale. *The American Journal of Psychiatry, 131*, 271–274.

Franklin, C., Trepper, T. S., Gingerich, W. J., & McCollum, E. E. (2012). *Solution-focused brief therapy: A handbook of evidence-based practice*. New York, NY: Oxford University Press.

Fredrickson, B. L., & Losoda, M. F. (2005). Positive affect and the complex dynamics of human flourishing. *American Psychologist, 60*, 678–686. http://doi.org/10.1037/0003-066X.60.7.678

Fredrickson, B. L. (2009). *Positivity.* New York, NY: Crown.

Furman, B., & Aloha, T. (2007). *Change through cooperation. Handbook of reteaming.* Helsinki, Finland: Helsinki Brief Therapy Institute.

Gable, S. L., Reis, H. T., Impett, E. A., & Asher, E. R. (2004). What do you do when things go right? The intrapersonal and interpersonal benefits of sharing positive events. *Journal of Personality and Social Psychology, 87*(2), 228–245. http://doi.org/10.1037/0022-3514.87.2.228

Ganis, G., Thompson, W. L., & Kosslyn, S. M. (2004). Brain areas underlying visual mental imagery and visual perception: An fMRI study. *Cognitive Brain Research, 20*, 116–241. http://doi.org/10.1016/j.cogbrainres.2004.02.012

Gilbert, P. (2010). *Compassion focused therapy.* New York, NY: Routledge.

Goldstein, N. J., Martin, D. J., & Cialdini, R. B. (2007). *Yes! 50 secrets from the science of persuasion.* London, UK: Profile Books.

Gollwitzer, P. M. (1999). Implementation intentions: Strong effects of simple plans. *American Psychologist, 54*(7), 493–503. http://doi.org/10.1037/0003-066X.54.7.493

Gottman, J. M. (1994). *What predicts divorce? The relationship between marital processes and marital outcomes.* New York, NY: Erlbaum.

Grant, A. M., & O'Connor, S.A. (2010). The differential effects of solution-focused and problem-focused coaching questions: A pilot study with implications for practice. *Industrial and Commercial Training, 42*(2), 102–111. http://doi.org/10.1108/00197851011026090

Grant Halvorson, H. (2010). *Succeed: How we can reach our goals.* London, UK: Penguin.

Hawkins, P., & Shohet, R. (2007). *Supervision in the helping professions.* Maidenhead, UK: McGraw-Hill.

Heath, A., & Tharp, L. (1991, October). *What therapists say about supervision.* Paper presented at the American Association for Marriage and Family Therapy Annual Conference, Dallas TX.

Heath, C., & Heath, D. (2010). *Switch. How to change things when change is hard.* New York, NY: Random House.

Hershberger, P. J. (2005). Prescribing happiness: Positive psychology and family medicine. *Family Medicine, 10*, 630–634.

Hiatt, D., & Hargrave, G. E. (1995). The characteristics of highly effective therapists in managed behavioral providers networks. *Behavioral Healthcare Tomorrow, 4*, 19–22.

Histed, M. H., Pasupathy, A., & Miller, E. K. (2009). Learning substrates in the primate prefrontal cortex and striatum: Sustained activity related to successful actions. *Neuron, 63*, 244–253. http://doi.org/10.1016/j.neuron.2009.06.019

Inskipp, F., & Proctor, B. (1993). *Making the most of supervision, Part I.* Twickenham, UK: Cascade Publications.

Inskipp, F., & Proctor, B. (1995) *The art, craft and tasks of counselling supervision, Part II: Becoming a supervisor.* Twickenham, UK: Cascade Publications.

Isen, A. M., Daubman, K. A., & Nowicki, G. P. (1987). Positive affect facilitates creative problem solving. *Journal of Personality and Social Psychology, 52*, 1122–1131. http://doi.org/10.1037/0022-3514.52.6.1122

Isen, A. M., Rosenzweig, A. S., & Young, M. J. (1991). The influence of positive affect on clinical problem solving. *Medical Decision Making, 11*, 331–337.

Isen, A. M., & Reeve, J. M. (2005). The Influence of positive affect on intrinsic and extrinsic motivation: Facilitating enjoyment of play, responsible work behavior, and self-control. *Motivation and Emotion, 29*(4), 297–325.

King, L. A. (2001). The health benefits of writing about life goals. *Personality and Social Psychology Bulletin, 27*, 798–807. http://doi.org/10.1177/0146167201277003

Kolb, D. A. (1984). *Experiential learning: Experience as the source of learning and development.* Engelwood Cliffs, NJ: Prentice Hall.

Lamarre, J., & Gregoire, A. (1999). Competence transfer in solution-focused therapy: Harnessing a natural resource. *Journal of Systemic Therapies, 18*(1), 43–57.

Leary, T. (1957). *Interpersonal diagnosis of personality.* New York, NY: Ronald.

Linden, van der, M. H. M. (1993). Ervaringen van supervisanten, wat weten we ervan? [Experiences of supervisees, what do we know about them?]. In H. M. van Praag & P. H. van Praag (Rev. ed.). *Handboek supervisie en intervisie in de psychotherapie* [Handbook of supervision and peer supervision in psychotherapy] (pp. 243–254). Amersfoort, The Netherlands: Academische uitgeverij.

Losada, M. F., & Heaphy, E. (2004). The role of positivity and connectivity in the performance of business teams: A nonlinear dynamics model. *American Behavioral Scientist, 47*(6), 740–765. http://doi.org/10.1177/0002764203260208

Lyubomirsky, S. (2008). *The how of happiness.* New York, NY: Pengiun.

Medina, A., & Beijebach, M. (2014). The impact of solution-focused training on professionals' beliefs, practices and burnout of child protection workers in Tenerife Island. *Child Care in Practice, 20*(1), 7–36. http://doi.org/10.1080/13575279.2013.847058

Menninger, K. (1959). The academic lecture: Hope. *The American Journal of Psychiatry, 12*, 481–491.

Metcalf, L. (1998). *Solution-focused group therapy.* New York, NY: Free Press.

Miller, S. D., Duncan, B. L., & Hubble, M. A. (1997). *Escape from Babel: Toward a unifying language for psychotherapy practice.* New York, NY: Norton.

Miller, S. D., Hubble, M. A., & Duncan, B. L. (1996). *The Handbook of solution-focused brief therapy: Foundations, applications, and research.* San Francisco, CA: Jossey-Bass.

Miller, T. (1995). *How to want what you have.* New York, NY: Avon.

Miller, W. R., & Rollnick, S. (2002). *Motivational interviewing. Preparing people for change* (*2nd ed.*). New York, NY: Guilford.

Moskowitz, S. A., & Rupert, P. A. (1983). Conflict resolution within the supervisory relationship. *Professional Psychology: Research and Practice, 14*, 632–641. http://doi.org/10.1037/0735-7028.14.5.632

Myers, D. G. (2000). Hope and happiness. In J. E. Gillham (Ed.), *The science of optimism and hope* (pp. 323–336). Philadelphia, PA: Templeton Foundation Press.

Neff, K. (2011). *Self-compassion.* New York, NY: HarperCollins.

Norcross, J. C. (2002). *Psychotherapy relationships that work; therapeutic contributions and responsiveness to patients* (Rev. ed.). Oxford, UK: University Press.

Norman, H. (2003). Solution-focused reflecting teams. In B. O'Connell & S. Palmer (Eds), *Handbook of solution-focused therapy* (pp. 156–167). London, UK: Sage.

Oettingen, G. (1999). Free fantasies about the future and the emergence of developmental goals. In J. Brandtstadter & R. M. Lerner (Eds.), *Action & self-development: Theory and research through the life span* (pp. 315–342). Thousand Oaks, CA: Sage.

Oettingen, G., Hönig, G., & Gollwitzer, P. M. (2000). Effective self-regulation of goal attainment. *International Journal of Educational Research, 33*, 705–732. http://doi.org/10.1016/S0883-0355(00)00046-X

Oettingen, G., Pak, H., & Schnetter, K. (2001). Self-regulation of goal setting: Turning free fantasies about the future into binding goals. *Journal of Personality and Social Psychology, 80*(5), 736–753. http://doi.org/10.1037/0022-3514.80.5.736

Oettingen, G., & Stephens, E.J. (2009). Fantasies and motivationally intelligent goal setting. In G. B. Moskowitz & H. Grant (Eds.), *The psychology of goals*. (pp. 153–178). New York, NY: Guilford.

O'Hanlon, B. (2000). *Do one thing different*. New York, NY: Quill, HarperCollins.

Orlemans, J. W. G., Eelen, P., & Hermans, D. (1995). *Inleiding tot de gedragstherapie* [Introduction to cognitive behavior therapy]. Houten, The Netherlands: Bohn Stafleu Van Loghum.

Orlinsky, D. E., & Ronnestad, M.H. (2005). *How psychotherapists develop: A study of therapeutic work and professional growth*. Washington DC: American Psychological Association.

Peacock, F. (2001). *Water the flowers, not the weeds*. Montreal, Canada: Open Heart.

Peterson, C. (2006). The Values in Action (VIA) classification of strengths: The un-DSM and the real DSM. In M. Csikszentmihalyi & I. Csikszentmihalyi (Eds.), *A life worth living: Contributions to positive psychology* (pp. 29–48). New York, NY: Oxford University Press.

Proctor, B., & Inskipp, F. (2001). Group supervision. In J. Scaife (Ed.). *Supervision in clinical practice* (pp. 99–121). London, UK: Routlegde.

Prochaska, J. O., Norcross, J. C., & DiClemente, C. C. (1994). *Changing for good*. New York, NY: Morrow.

Roeden, J. M., & Bannink, F. P. (2007). *Handboek oplossingsgericht werken met licht verstandelijk beperkte cliënten* [Handbook solution-focused interviewing with clients with intellectual disabilities]. Amsterdam, The Netherlands: Pearson.

Ross, M. & Wilson, A. E. (2002). It feels like yesterday: Self-esteem, valence of personal past experiences, and judgements of subjective distance. *Journal of Personality and Social Psychology, 82,* 792–803. http://doi.org/10.1037/0022-3514.82.5.792

Rossi, E. L. (Ed.) (1980). *The nature of hypnosis and suggestions by Milton Erickson (collected papers)*. New York, NY: Irvington.

Rothman, A. J. (2000). Toward a theory-based analysis of behavioral maintenance. *Health Psychology, 19,* 64–69. http://doi.org/10.1037/0278-6133.19.Suppl1.64

Rudes, J., Shilts, L., & Berg, I. K. (1997). Focused supervision seen through a recursive frame analysis. *Journal of Marital and Family Therapy, 23*(2), 203–215. http://doi.org/10.1111/j.1752-0606.1997.tb00244.x

Saint-Exupery, A. de (1979). *The wisdom of the sands*. Chicago, IL: University of Chicago.

Selekman, M. D., & Todd, T. C. (1995). Cocreating a context for change in the supervisory system: The solution-focused supervision model. *Journal of Systemic Therapies, 14,* 21–22.

Selekman, M. D. (1997). *Solution focused therapy with children*. New York, NY: Guilford.

Seligman, M. E. P. (2002). *Authentic happiness*. New York, NY: Free Press.

Seligman, M. E. P., Steen, T. A., Park, N., & Peterson, C. (2005). Positive psychology progress: Empirical validation of interventions. *American Psycholoist, 60*(5), 410–421. http://doi.org/10.1037/0003-066X.60.5.410

Seligman, M. E. P. (2011). *Flourish.* New York, NY: Free Press.

Shanfield, S. B., Matthews, K. L., & Hetherly, V. (1993). What do excellent psychotherapy supervisors do? *American Journal of Psychiatry, 150,* 1081–1084.

Snyder, C. R. (1994). *The psychology of hope: You can get there from here*. New York, NY: Free Press.

Snyder, C. R., Michael, S. T., & Cheavens, J. (1999). Hope as a psychotherapeutic foundation of common factors, placebos and expectancies. In M. A. Hubble, B. Duncan, & S. Miller (Eds.), *The heart and soul of change*, (pp. 257–276). Washington, DC: American Psychological Association.

Thomas, F. (1996). Solution-focused supervision: The coaxing of expertise. In S. D. Miller, M. A. Hubble, & B. L. Duncan. (Eds.), *Handbook of solution-focused brief therapy* (pp. 128–151). San Francisco, CA: Jossey-Bass.

Triantafillou, N. (1997). A solution-focused approach to mental health supervision. *Journal of Systemic Therapies*, 16(4), 305–328. Veeninga, A. (2008). Supervisie in de opleiding tot cognitief gedragstherapeut [Supervision in the training to become a cognitive behavioral therapist]. *Gedragstherapie, 41*(4), 367–371.

Veeninga, A., & Hafkenscheid, A. (2010). Persoonsgerichte supervisie in de psychotherapie opleiding [Personal supervision in psychotherapy]. *Tijdschrift voor Psychotherapie, 36*, 108–119. http://doi.org/10.1007/BF03096128

Visser, C. F. (2012). *How the solution-focusedness of coaches is related to their thriving at work*. Retrieved from http://www.m-cc.nl/How%20the%20solution-focusedness%20of%20coaches%20is%20related%20to%20their%20thriving%20at%20work.pdf

Walter, J. L., & Peller, J. E. (1992). *Becoming solution-focused in brief therapy*. New York, NY: Brunner/Mazel.

Walter, J. L., & Peller, J. E. (2000). *Recreating brief therapy, preferences and possibilities*. New York, NY: Norton.

Wampold, B. E. (2001). *The great psychotherapy debate: Models, methods, and findings*. New York, NY: Erlbaum.

Wampold, B. E., & Bathi, K. S. (2004). Attending to the omissions: A historical examination of evidence-based practice movements. *Professional Psychology: Research and Practice, 35*(6), 563–570. http://doi.org/10.1037/0735-7028.35.6.563

Watkins, C. E. (Ed.) (1997). *The handbook of psychotherapy supervision*. New York, NY: Wiley.

Watkins, C. E. (1998). Psychotherapy supervision in the 21st century: Some pressing needs and impressing possibilities. *Journal of Psychotherapy Practice and Research, 7*, 93–101.

Watzlawick, P., Weakland, J. H., & Fisch, R. (1974). *Change: Principles of problem formation and problem resolution*. New York: Norton

Webster Nelson, D. (2009). Feeling good and open-minded: The impact of positive affect on cross cultural empathic responding. *The Journal of Positive Psychology, 4*(1), 53–63. http://doi.org/10.1080/17439760802357859

Wei-Su, H. (2008, March). *Study of the components of solution-focused supervision*. Paper presented at the meeting of International Counseling Psychology Conference, Chicago.

Williams, L .A., & DeSteno, D. (2008). Pride and perseverance: The motivational role of pride. *Journal of Personality and Social Psychology, 94*(6), 1007–1017. http://doi.org/10.1037/0022-3514.94.6.1007

Wiseman, R. (2009). *59 seconds. Think a little change a lot.* London, UK: Pan Books.

Wittgenstein, L. (1968). *Philosophical investigations* (G.E.M. Anscombe, translation, 3rd ed.). New York, NY: Macmillan.

Worthen, V., & McNeill, B. (1996). A phenomenological investigation of "good supervision events." *Journal of Counseling Psychology, 43*, 25–34. http://doi.org/10.1037/0022-0167.43.1.25

Websites

www.asfct.org
Association for the Quality Development of Solution Focused Consulting and Training (SFCT)

www.authentichappiness.org
Seligman with positive psychology questionnaires

www.brief.org.uk
BRIEF London

www.brieftherapysydney.com.au
Brief Therapy Institute of Sydney, Australia

www.brief-therapy.org
Brief Family Therapy Center: founders of solution-focused brief therapy (SFBT)

www.centerforclinicalexcellence.com
International Center for Clinical Excellence (ICCE), worldwide community dedicated to promote excellence in behavioural healthcare services (S.D. Miller)

www.ebta.nu
European Brief Therapy Association (EBTA)

www.edwdebono.com
Edward de Bono, author

www.enpp.eu
European Network for Positive Psychology (ENPP)

www.fredrickson.socialpsychology.org
Fredrickson, research broaden and build theory of positive emotions

www.fredrikebannink.com
Author of this book

www.gingerich.net
Gingerich, research SFBT

www.heartandsoulofchange.com
Duncan, author

www.heidigranthalvorson.com
Grant Halvorson, researcher compliments

www.ippanetwork.org
Institute Positive Psychology Association (IPPA)

www.positivepsychology.org
Pennsylvania University with questionnaires

www.posttraumatic-success.com
Bannink, author Post Traumatic Success

www.pos-cbt.com
Bannink, author Practicing Positive CBT

www.ppc.sas.upenn.edu/ppquestionnaires.htm
Penn University with positive psychology questionnaires

www.reteaming.com
Furman, author

www.scottdmiller.com
Miller with Session Rating Scale (SRS) and Group Rating Scale (GRS)

www.sfbta.org
Solution-Focused Brief Therapy Association (SFBTA)

www.solutionsdoc.co.uk
Macdonald, research SFBT

www.solworld.org
Solutions in Organisations Link (SOL), solution-focused coaching and management

www.ted.com
Talks about Technology, Entertainment, and Design (TED)

Appendices

Appendix 1: The Positive Supervision Process

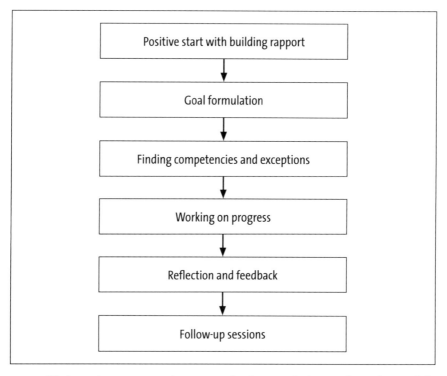

- If there is progress: do more of what works/stop when the goal is reached;
- If there is no progress: stop and do something different: return to building rapport and/or goal formulation and start the process again/stop/ refer.

The positive supervision process is carried out for the entire supervision and/ or for each supervision session individually.

Appendix 2: Protocols for the First Session

Protocol 1

Submit all questions to all supervisees present

Building Rapport

Problem
"What brings you here?"; "How is that a problem for you?"; "What have you already tried that has been useful?"

Goal Formulation
"What would you like to be different as a result of the supervision?" Here the supervisor may ask the *miracle question* (see Chapter 3) or other questions about goal formulation.

Exceptions
"When have you caught a glimpse of this miracle?"; "How did you make that happen?" Alternatively: "When is the problem absent or less noticeable?"; "How do you manage to do that?"; "Which personal strengths and resources do you use?"

Scaling
Progress: "Where are you now on a scale of progress of 10–0?"; "How do you manage to be at that point (and not lower)?"

Motivation: "Where are you now on a scale of 10–0, if 10 means you're willing to give it your all and 0 means you're not willing to put in any effort?"

Confidence: "Where are you now on a scale of 10–0, if 10 means that you are very confident and 0 means you have no confidence at all that you can reach your goal?"

Concluding the Session

- If the supervisees give a concrete and detailed description of their miracle or another question about goal formulation, suggest: "Pick a day in the coming week, pretend the miracle has happened, and observe what difference that makes."
- If the supervisees do not give a concrete and detailed response to the miracle question or another question about goal formulation, suggest: "Pay attention to what happens in your life that you gives you the sense

that this problem can be solved." Or alternatively: "Pay attention to what is happening in your life that you would like to keep happening because it is good (enough)."

- Ask the supervisees if they think is it useful to return. If so, ask: "When would you like to return?"

Feedback From Supervisees *(see Chapter 6 and Appendix 6).*

Protocol 2

Submit all questions to all supervisees present

Building Rapport

Ask the Four Basic Solution-Focused Questions
1. "What are your best hopes (for this supervision)?"; "What else?"
2. "What difference will that make?"; "What else will be different?"
3. "What is working?"; "What else is working?"
4. "What will be next signs of progress?" or "What will be your next step?"; "What else?"

Concluding the Session (see protocol 1)

Feedback From Supervisees

Sometimes supervisees cannot answer all four questions during the first supervision session, because asking: *What else* usually takes some time. The next session the supervisors and supervisees continue with one of the protocols for the first session. Supervisees may also think about these questions (e.g., question 3 and 4) as a homework suggestion.

Appendix 3: Protocol for Finding Exceptions

As you look for exceptions, you may inquire about the supervisees' observations and, using the *interactional matrix* (see Appendix 5), about what others who are important to the supervisee might be able to perceive.

You may distinguish between exceptions pertaining to the desired outcome (the goal) and exceptions pertaining to the problem.

Submit all questions to all supervisees present.

Exceptions Pertaining to the Goal

Elicit. "So, when your goal has been reached (or the miracle has happened), you will feel relaxed, even with dominant clients."; "When do you already see glimpses of that?"; "If such a client were here and I asked him or her what they notice that is different about you, what do you think (s)he would say?"

Amplify. "When was the last time you felt a bit more relaxed when seeing a dominant client? Please tell me more about that."; "What was different?"; "What else was different about that time?"; "What did you do differently?"; "How did the client react to that?"

Reinforce. Nonverbal: Lean forward, raise your eyebrows, or make notes (do what you naturally do when someone tells you something important). Verbal: Show interest. "Was this new for you? Did it surprise you that this happened?" Give acknowledgment and pay compliments: "It seems that it was pretty difficult and that it required courage for you to do that. I am correct?"

Explore. "What do you think you did differently to make that happen?"; "Did the client react in a different way?"; "And how was this different for you?" Pay compliments: "Where did you get the great idea to do it that way? What great ideas you have!"; "Are you someone who often comes up with the right ideas at the right time?"

Project exceptions into the future. "On a scale of 10–0, where 10 means a very good chance and 0 means no chance at all, how do you rate the chances of something like that happening again in the coming week (or month)?"; "What would it take?"; "What or who could help you to have that happen more often in the future?";

"What is the most important thing you need to keep remembering to make sure this has the best chance of happening again?"

Exceptions Pertaining to the Problem

Ask about exceptions. If the supervisee cannot describe a goal (or miracle) and talks only in problem terms, say: "Please recall a time in the past week (or month, or year) when the problem was less severe, or when the problem was absent for a short period of time." Then continue with the five steps for exceptions pertaining to the goal (or miracle).

Ask about progress. All subsequent sessions commence with the exploration of positive differences. Ask: "What is better since the last time we met?" Remember to follow all five steps and to ask both individual and relational (interactional matrix) questions. After examining an exception, always start again by asking: "What else is better?"

Ask coping questions. Sometimes the supervisees are unable to find exceptions and the difficulties they face are enormous. In that case, you may ask coping questions to find out what the supervisees do to keep their head above water: "I'm surprised. Given everything that's happened, I don't know how you cope. How do you do that? Which of your personal strengths do you use? How do you keep your head above water?"

Give acknowledgment. If the supervisees describe a prolonged unpleasant situation with ever-discouraging events, you might say: "I understand that you have many reasons to be down. There are so many things that turned out differently than you'd hoped. I wonder how you've kept going and how you've been able to get up every morning and start a new day. Please tell me more."

Use positive character interpretations. If the supervisees say they must go on, for example, for their clients' sake, you might say: "Is that how you do it? You think of your clients and how much they need you? You must be a really caring person. Please tell me more about what you do to take good care of them."

Appendix 4: Protocol for Follow-Up Sessions

Submit all questions to each client present.
   Use EARS (see Chapter 7):

Eliciting. "What is better (since the previous session)?"

Amplifying (asking for details). "How does that work?"; "How do you do that exactly?"; "Is that new for you?"; "What effect does this have on….?"; "What is different between you and ….?"

Reinforcing. Give the supervisees compliments and competence questions.

Start again. "What else is better?"

Scaling progress. "Where are you now on the scale?"; "How did you make that happen?"; "What does one point higher look like?"; "What will be different then?"; "What will you be doing differently?"; "What or who may help you to get to one point higher?"; "Who will be the first to notice?"; "How would that person notice?"; "How will (s)he react?", "What difference will that make for you?"; "At what point on the scale would you like to end up?"

If useful: scale motivation, hope, and confidence
   • *Homework suggestions*. If the supervisees want to do homework, behavioral tasks may be given to supervisees in a customer relationship, observational tasks for supervisees in a complainant relationship, and no tasks for supervisees in a visitor relationship (see Chapter 8).
   • *Concluding the session.* "Do you think it is useful for you to return?" If so: "When would you like to return?"
   • *Feedback from supervisees*

Appendix 5: Interactional Matrix

The interactional matrix uses questions from three different perspectives: the self, an other, and a third person (observer). The matrix is useful in many different situations, as described in this book. The three questions from the interactional matrix are also useful if there is a complainant relationship between the supervisees and their clients, or if there is a complainant relationship between the supervisors and their supervisees (see Chapter 8).

Ask supervisees (or yourself as a supervisor) to answer the following three questions from the interactional matrix, ensuring you use this sequence:
1. When this problem is solved, what will you notice is different about the other person? What will you see him/her doing differently? What else? What else?
2. When this problem is solved, what will this other person notice is different about you? What will this other person see you doing differently? What else? What else?
3. When this problem is solved and you are being watched by an outside observer, what will this person notice is different about your relationship with the other person? What will this observer see both of you doing differently? What else? What else?

Appendix 6: Session Rating Scale (SRS)

Session Rating Scale (SRS V.3.0)

Name _____ Age (Yrs):_____

ID# _____ Sex: M / F

Session # _____ Date: _____

Please rate today's session by placing a mark on the line nearest to the description that best fits your experience.

Relationship

I did not feel heard, understood, and respected. |——————————————| I felt heard, understood, and respected.

Goals and Topics

We did not work on or talk about what I wanted to work on and talk about. |——————————————| We worked on and talked about what I wanted to work on and talk about.

Approach or Method

The therapist's approach is not a good fit for me. |——————————————| The therapist's approach is a good fit for me.

Overall

There was something missing in the session today. |——————————————| Overall, today's session was right for me.

Appendix 7: Questionnaire for (Assessing) Supervisors

Below is a questionnaire for (assessing) supervisors, which is based, first and foremost, on what is most important in supervision: the supervisees' perspective (see Chapter 1).

1. What would your supervisees say you do to help them to function optimally?
2. What else would they say? And what else?
3. What difference do your supervisees say you make for them?
4. What would your supervisees say about how useful the sessions have been so far on a scale from 10–0 (10 is the most useful and 0 is the opposite)?
5. What would they say about their rating of the usefulness of the supervision (and why they don't rate the usefulness lower)?
6. What would they say will be different and what would they say you will be doing differently at one or two points higher on that scale?
7. How can you get higher on the scale according to them?
8. What would they say has been most useful and helpful in your work with them?

Appendix 8: Proposal to Change an Assessment Form for Prospective Supervisors

This is a proposal to change an assessment form used in the screening of prospective supervisors. The form is currently used by the Dutch Association for Behavioural and Cognitive Therapies (VGCt) to assess whether a member of the Association, who applies to become a supervisor, may be admitted. In order for the applicant to become a supervisor (s)he needs to have two positive references by other supervisors who are members of the Association. Until now these two colleagues have had to fill out a form whose focus was solely on problems. The questions are all aimed at what the applicant might find wrong with supervisees and their handling of clients; they are aimed at giving advice, giving interpretations, and making hypotheses; they all focus on what is not working, negative emotions, uncertainties, weaknesses, and deficits of the supervisees.

To offer an overview on how a more positive focus can be used, the current form is placed on the left side of the table. To indicate how this may be changed, using the positive supervision point of view, the alterations are placed on the right side of the table (see Table 6). This form will simultaneously make clear how positive supervision is different from traditional supervision and how the two visions can be easily combined. It is hoped that in the future the positive focus in supervision will replace the purely negative one, which to date has often been used.

1. Where were you working when you met the applicant? When was this?
2. Would you refer supervisees to the applicant? If so, why? If not: why not?
3. Are the following statements in your opinion applicable?

Table 6. Assessment form for prospective supervisors

Traditional supervision	Positive supervision
The applicant will treat the supervisees as equals.	Unchanged
The applicant will listen and be open to the ideas of the supervisees.	Unchanged
The applicant will provide advice, suggestions, and interpretations regarding the clients of the supervisees.	The applicant understands that supervision is first and foremost about the supervisees and how they cooperate optimally with their clients, and that the

Table 6. continued

	applicant doesn't need to know much about the clients of the supervisees. The applicant will only provide advice after the supervisees have brought up their own ideas and competencies and only after being invited to do so. The applicant will not make interpretations (or make hypotheses).
The applicant will provide advice, suggestions, and interpretations regarding a formulated goal.	The applicant will ask the supervisees how they learn best. If the supervisees learn best when receiving advice and suggestions, the applicant will adjust to their wishes. The applicant will only provide advice or suggestions ater the supervisees have brought up their own ideas and competencies and only after being invited to do so. The applicant will not make interpretations.
The applicant will motivate the supervisees as much as possible to address and solve problems, especially in the first part of the supervision process.	The applicant will motivate the supervisees as much as possible to address and solve problems, though they will work mainly to address and build the supervisees' strengths and successes and continue to do this building during the entire supervision process.
The applicant will encourage the supervisees to discuss emotional issues with regard to the process between therapist and client.	The applicant will encourage the supervisees to discuss positive emotional issues with regard to the process between therapist and client though negative issues may be touched on.
The applicant will create an atmosphere which encourages the supervisees to develop as therapists and discuss and solve any uncertainties they have about their role.	The applicant will create an atmosphere which encourages the supervisees to develop as therapists and enhance their skills. This includes first discussing with them the areas where they have confidence and then if required those where there is some uncertainty.

Table 6. continued

The applicant will give feedback to the supervisees in a way which stimulates them.	The applicant will give feedback to the supervisees in a way which stimulates them and will also ask for feedback from the supervisees in return.
The applicant will be creative enough to ask extensively about what is going wrong in the supervisee's treatments.	The applicant will be creative enough to ask extensively about what is going right in the supervisee's treatments.
The applicant will not impose on the supervisees, his/her own norms and values in doing therapy.	The applicant will give directives if needed, when there is danger, risk, or unethical behavior on the part of the supervisees.
The applicant will distinguish different stages in the supervision process (from technical to more personal).	The applicant will understand that the supervision process intermingles both technical and personal aspects of therapy and the supervisees are seen as coexperts from the start.
The applicant will acknowledge and discuss the personal deficits of the supervisees.	The applicant will acknowledge first and foremost the personal strengths and competencies of the supervisees and if necessary also discuss any perceived personal deficits.
The applicant will motivate the supervisees to try new solutions and new interventions when they are fairly advanced in their methods.	Because the supervisees are always seen as coexperts, the applicant will motivate the supervisees, from the start of the supervision, to try new solutions and new interventions.
The applicant is capable of sharing knowledge.	Unchanged
The applicant knows how to create enthusiasm for cognitive behavioral therapy in the supervisees.	Unchanged
The applicant is aware of recent developments in cognitive behavioral therapy.	Unchanged

4. Did the applicant, as far as you know, undergo peer supervision during the last three years?
5. Do you know if the applicant has been active in attending conferences, workshops etc?
6. In your opinion what are the strengths of the applicant as a cognitive behavioral therapist?
7. In your opinion what are the weaknesses of the applicant as a cognitive behavioral therapist?
    In the positive form this is replaced by: *In your opinion what are the competencies the applicant may (or should) develop further as a cognitive behavioral therapist?*
8. Based on your answers above, would you recommend the applicant as a supervisor for the Dutch Association for Behavioural and Cognitive Therapies (VGCt)?

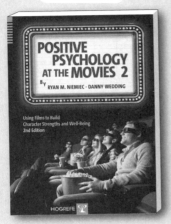